Every

Commandment

of

Jesus Christ

in the

Holy Bible

Every Commandment of Jesus Christ In The Holy Bible

This book is brought to you by followers of Jesus Christ
with the shared motive of; making the Commandments of Jesus Christ
known to all nations and uniting the followers of Jesus Christ globally.

Published by United In Jesus Christ

A Not-For-Profit Organization

www.UnitedInJesusChrist.org

Publisher's Cataloging-in-Publication data

Names: United In Jesus Christ, author.

Title: Every Commandment of Jesus Christ in the Holy Bible /
United In Jesus Christ.

Description: Yucaipa, CA: United In Jesus Christ, 2021.

Identifiers: LCCN: 2021913776 | ISBN: 978-1-7373805-3-5 (hardcover) |
978-1-7373805-0-4 (large print) | 978-1-7373805-1-1 (paperback) |
978-1-7373805-7-3 (ebook) | 978-1-7373805-9-7 (audio)

Subjects: LCSH Jesus Christ--Teachings. | Bible. New Testament. | Bible. New
Testament--Textbooks. | Bible--Handbooks, manuals, etc. | Christian life. |
BISAC RELIGION / Biblical Reference / Handbooks | RELIGION / Biblical
Studies / New Testament / General | RELIGION / Christian Living / Devotional

Classification: LCC BS2415.A2 U65 2021 | DDC 232.9/54--dc23

First Edition: 2021 | 5781

TABLE OF CONTENTS

PREFACE

This book has been produced **without** bias or denominational influence or interest.

This book contains every canonized commandment of Jesus Christ since He came as a man found in the King James Version of the Holy Bible.

The word **Commandment** is defined as; **an authoritative order**.

•Judgments and General announcements of Jesus Christ are not included in this book.

•Commandments of Jesus Christ that are not direct quotes are not included in this book.

•No commandments that have both the same phraseology and context are repeated in this book.

•Only Commandments that the Holy Bible makes definitively clear were spoken by Jesus Christ Himself are included in this book.

Jesus is recorded in the Holy Bible saying a wide range of Commandments. We did not take it upon ourselves to exclude any of His commandments from this book. Instead, we have been intentional to provide a comprehensive publication of all the Commandments of Jesus Christ in the Holy Bible without discretion (per the stated criteria).

This book is not a substitute for the Holy Bible.

This book is a tool to help you become a disciple of Jesus Christ and to help you help others to become disciples of Jesus Christ as well.

Knowing and Living the Commandments of Jesus
Christ is essential to our walk with Him. As followers
of Jesus Christ learn of Him and Live His Word,
genuine unity among His followers can manifest.

The Mission of United In Jesus Christ is the Unity that
Jesus Christ prayed for recorded in The Gospel
According To John chapter 17.

*"As thou hast sent me into the world, even so have
I also sent them into the world. And for their sakes
I sanctify myself, that they also might be sanctified
through the truth. Neither pray I for these alone, but for
them also which shall believe on me through their word;*
**That they all may be one; as thou, Father, art in me,
and I in thee, that they also may be one in us: that the
world may believe that thou hast sent me. And the
glory which thou gavest me I have given them; that
they may be one, even as we are one: I in them, and
thou in me, that they may be made perfect in one; and
that the world may know that thou hast sent me, and
hast loved them, as thou hast loved me.***"
John 17:18-23

Followers of Jesus Christ today have a variety of
backgrounds, doctrinal understandings, and practices
but we can all find common ground in the teachings of
Jesus Christ recorded in the Holy Bible. When we all
know what the Holy Bible records that Jesus
Commanded His followers, then all who will do as He,
our leader says will have Jesus Christ and His Word to
be United in. Unity in a common understanding and
lifestyle continuing in the teaching and commandments
of Jesus Christ. The commandments of our Master,
Teacher, and Friend Jesus Christ is what ALL His
followers can find common ground in.

Jesus commanded:
*"If ye love me, **keep my commandments.**"*
John 14:15

Jesus also commanded His disciples to:
*"**Go ye therefore, and teach all nations,** baptizing them in the name of the Father, and of the Son, and of the Holy Ghost: **Teaching them to observe all things whatsoever I have commanded you:** and, lo, I am with you always, even unto the end of the world. Amen."*
Matthew 28:19-20

Jesus commanded His disciples to Keep His Commandments if they Love Him. Also, part of what Jesus commanded His disciples to do is teach all nations to observe **all things** whatsoever He has **commanded** them. With this in mind, knowing, living, and teaching the Commandments of Jesus Christ is **essential** to a life of following Him.

1 John 2:1-6
"My little children, these things write I unto you, that ye sin not. And if any man sin, we have an advocate with the Father, Jesus Christ the righteous: And he is the propitiation for our sins: and not for ours only, but also for the sins of the whole world. And **hereby we do know that we know him, if we keep his commandments. He that saith, I know him, and keepeth not his commandments, is a liar, and the truth is not in him. But whoso keepeth his word, in him verily is the love of God perfected: hereby know we that we are in him. He that saith he abideth in him ought himself also so to walk, even as he walked.**"

Commandments
of Jesus Christ
found in:

THE GOSPEL
ACCORDING
TO
MATTHEW

Number	Commandment	Context of Commandment
1	*Suffer it to be so now: for thus it becometh us to fulfil all righteousness.*	Matthew 3:13-17 Then cometh Jesus from Galilee to Jordan unto John, to be baptized of him. But John forbad him, saying, I have need to be baptized of thee, and comest thou to me? And Jesus answering said unto him, **Suffer it to be so now: for thus it becometh us to fulfil all righteousness.** Then he suffered him. And Jesus, when he was baptized, went up straightway out of the water: and, lo, the heavens were opened unto him, and he saw the Spirit of God descending like a dove, and lighting upon him: And lo a voice from heaven, saying, This is my beloved Son, in whom I am well pleased.
2	*Get thee hence, Satan:*	Matthew 4:8-11 Again, the devil taketh him up into an exceeding high mountain, and sheweth him all the kingdoms of the world, and the glory of them; And saith unto him, All these things will I give thee, if thou wilt fall down and worship me. Then saith Jesus unto him, **Get thee hence, Satan:** for it is written, Thou shalt worship the Lord thy God, and him only shalt thou serve. Then the devil leaveth him, and, behold, angels came and ministered unto him.
3	*Repent: for the kingdom of heaven is at hand.*	Matthew 4:12-17 Now when Jesus had heard that John was cast into prison, he departed into Galilee; And leaving Nazareth, he came and dwelt in Capernaum, which is upon the sea coast, in the borders of Zabulon and Nephthalim: That it might be fulfilled which was spoken by Esaias the prophet, saying, The land of Zabulon, and the land of Nephthalim, by the way of the sea, beyond Jordan, Galilee of the Gentiles; The people which sat in darkness saw great light, and to them which sat in the region and shadow of death light is sprung up. From that time Jesus began to preach, and to say, **Repent: for the kingdom of heaven is at hand.**

Number	Commandment	Context of Commandment
4	*Follow me, and I will make you fishers of men.*	Matthew 4:18-22 And Jesus, walking by the sea of Galilee, saw two brethren, Simon called Peter, and Andrew his brother, casting a net into the sea: for they were fishers. And he saith unto them, **Follow me, and I will make you fishers of men.** And they straightway left their nets, and followed him. And going on from thence, he saw other two brethren, James the son of Zebedee, and John his brother, in a ship with Zebedee their father, mending their nets; and he called them. And they immediately left the ship and their father, and followed him.
5	*Rejoice, and be exceeding glad: for great is your reward in heaven: for so persecuted they the prophets which were before you.*	Matthew 5:10-12 Blessed are they which are persecuted for righteousness' sake: for theirs is the kingdom of heaven. Blessed are ye, when men shall revile you, and persecute you, and shall say all manner of evil against you falsely, for my sake. **Rejoice, and be exceeding glad: for great is your reward in heaven: for so persecuted they the prophets which were before you.**
6	*Let your light so shine before men, that they may see your good works, and glorify your Father which is in heaven.*	Matthew 5:14-16 Ye are the light of the world. A city that is set on an hill cannot be hid. Neither do men light a candle, and put it under a bushel, but on a candlestick; and it giveth light unto all that are in the house. **Let your light so shine before men, that they may see your good works, and glorify your Father which is in heaven.**

4

Number	Commandment	Context of Commandment

Matthew 5:17-20
Think not that I am come to destroy the law, or the prophets: I am not come to destroy, but to fulfil. For verily I say unto you, Till heaven and earth pass, one jot or one tittle shall in no wise pass from the law, till all be fulfilled. Whosoever therefore shall break one of these least commandments, and shall teach men so, he shall be called the least in the kingdom of heaven: but whosoever shall do and teach them, the same shall be called great in the kingdom of heaven. For I say unto you, That except your righteousness shall exceed the righteousness of the scribes and Pharisees, ye shall in no case enter into the kingdom of heaven.

7 — *Think not that I am come to destroy the law, or the prophets: I am not come to destroy, but to fulfil.*

Matthew 5:21-24
Ye have heard that it was said of them of old time, Thou shalt not kill; and whosoever shall kill shall be in danger of the judgment: But I say unto you, That whosoever is angry with his brother without a cause shall be in danger of the judgment: and whosoever shall say to his brother, Raca, shall be in danger of the council: but whosoever shall say, Thou fool, shall be in danger of hell fire. Therefore **if thou bring thy gift to the altar, and there rememberest that thy brother hath ought against thee; Leave there thy gift before the altar, and go thy way; first be reconciled to thy brother, and then come and offer thy gift.**

8 — *if thou bring thy gift to the altar, and there rememberest that thy brother hath ought against thee; Leave there thy gift before the altar, and go thy way; first be reconciled to thy brother, and then come and offer thy gift.*

Number	Commandment	Context of Commandment
9	*Agree with thine adversary quickly, whiles thou art in the way with him; lest at any time the adversary deliver thee to the judge, and the judge deliver thee to the officer, and thou be cast into prison.*	Matthew 5:25-26 **Agree with thine adversary quickly, whiles thou art in the way with him; lest at any time the adversary deliver thee to the judge, and the judge deliver thee to the officer, and thou be cast into prison.** Verily I say unto thee, Thou shalt by no means come out thence, till thou hast paid the uttermost farthing.
10	*if thy right eye offend thee, pluck it out, and cast it from thee: for it is profitable for thee that one of thy members should perish, and not that thy whole body should be cast into hell.*	Matthew 5:27-29 Ye have heard that it was said by them of old time, Thou shalt not commit adultery: But I say unto you, That whosoever looketh on a woman to lust after her hath committed adultery with her already in his heart. And **if thy right eye offend thee, pluck it out, and cast it from thee: for it is profitable for thee that one of thy members should perish, and not that thy whole body should be cast into hell.**
11	*if thy right hand offend thee, cut it off, and cast it from thee: for it is profitable for thee that one of thy members should perish, and not that thy whole body should be cast into hell.*	Matthew 5:30 And **if thy right hand offend thee, cut it off, and cast it from thee: for it is profitable for thee that one of thy members should perish, and not that thy whole body should be cast into hell.**

Commandments of Jesus Christ found in: The Gospel According To Matthew

Number	Commandment	Context of Commandment
12	*Swear not at all; neither by heaven; for it is God's throne: Nor by the earth; for it is his footstool: neither by Jerusalem; for it is the city of the great King. Neither shalt thou swear by thy head, because thou canst not make one hair white or black.*	Matthew 5:33-36 Again, ye have heard that it hath been said by them of old time, Thou shalt not forswear thyself, but shalt perform unto the Lord thine oaths: But I say unto you, **Swear not at all; neither by heaven; for it is God's throne: Nor by the earth; for it is his footstool: neither by Jerusalem; for it is the city of the great King. Neither shalt thou swear by thy head, because thou canst not make one hair white or black.**
13	*let your communication be, Yea, yea; Nay, nay: for whatsoever is more than these cometh of evil.*	Matthew 5:37 But **let your communication be, Yea, yea; Nay, nay: for whatsoever is more than these cometh of evil.**
14	*resist not evil:*	Matthew 5:38-39 Ye have heard that it hath been said, An eye for an eye, and a tooth for a tooth: But I say unto you, That ye **resist not evil**: but whosoever shall smite thee on thy right cheek, turn to him the other also.
15	*whosoever shall smite thee on thy right cheek, turn to him the other also.*	Matthew 5:39 But I say unto you, That ye resist not evil: but **whosoever shall smite thee on thy right cheek, turn to him the other also.**

Number	Commandment	Context of Commandment
16	*if any man will sue thee at the law, and take away thy coat, let him have thy cloak also.*	Matthew 5:40 And **if any man will sue thee at the law, and take away thy coat, let him have thy cloak also.**
17	*whosoever shall compel thee to go a mile, go with him twain.*	Matthew 5:41 And **whosoever shall compel thee to go a mile, go with him twain.**
18	*Give to him that asketh thee,*	Matthew 5:42 **Give to him that asketh thee,** and from him that would borrow of thee turn not thou away.
19	*from him that would borrow of thee turn not thou away.*	Matthew 5:42 Give to him that asketh thee, and **from him that would borrow of thee turn not thou away.**
20	*Love your enemies,*	Matthew 5:43-44 Ye have heard that it hath been said, Thou shalt love thy neighbour, and hate thine enemy. But I say unto you, **Love your enemies,** bless them that curse you, do good to them that hate you, and pray for them which despitefully use you, and persecute you;
21	*bless them that curse you,*	Matthew 5:44 But I say unto you, Love your enemies, **bless them that curse you,** do good to them that hate you, and pray for them which despitefully use you, and persecute you;

8

Number	Commandment	Context of Commandment
22	*do good to them that hate you,*	Matthew 5:44 But I say unto you, Love your enemies, bless them that curse you, **do good to them that hate you,** and pray for them which despitefully use you, and persecute you;
23	*pray for them which despitefully use you, and persecute you;*	Matthew 5:44-45 But I say unto you, Love your enemies, bless them that curse you, do good to them that hate you, and **pray for them which despitefully use you, and persecute you**; That ye may be the children of your Father which is in heaven: for he maketh his sun to rise on the evil and on the good, and sendeth rain on the just and on the unjust.
24	*Be ye therefore perfect, even as your Father which is in heaven is perfect.*	Matthew 5:46-48 For if ye love them which love you, what reward have ye? do not even the publicans the same? And if ye salute your brethren only, what do ye more than others? do not even the publicans so? **Be ye therefore perfect, even as your Father which is in heaven is perfect.**
25	*Take heed that ye do not your alms before men, to be seen of them:*	Matthew 6:1 **Take heed that ye do not your alms before men, to be seen of them:** otherwise ye have no reward of your Father which is in heaven.
26	*when thou doest thine alms, do not sound a trumpet before thee, as the hypocrites do in the synagogues and in the streets, that they may have glory of men.*	Matthew 6:2 Therefore **when thou doest thine alms, do not sound a trumpet before thee, as the hypocrites do in the synagogues and in the streets, that they may have glory of men.** Verily I say unto you, They have their reward.

Number	Commandment	Context of Commandment
27	*when thou doest alms, let not thy left hand know what thy right hand doeth:*	Matthew 6:3-4 But **when thou doest alms, let not thy left hand know what thy right hand doeth:** That thine alms may be in secret: and thy Father which seeth in secret himself shall reward thee openly.
28	*when thou prayest, thou shalt not be as the hypocrites are:*	Matthew 6:5 And **when thou prayest, thou shalt not be as the hypocrites are:** for they love to pray standing in the synagogues and in the corners of the streets, that they may be seen of men. Verily I say unto you, They have their reward.
29	*when thou prayest, enter into thy closet, and when thou hast shut thy door, pray to thy Father which is in secret;*	Matthew 6:6 But thou, **when thou prayest, enter into thy closet, and when thou hast shut thy door, pray to thy Father which is in secret;** and thy Father which seeth in secret shall reward thee openly.
30	*when ye pray, use not vain repetitions, as the heathen do: for they think that they shall be heard for their much speaking. Be not ye therefore like unto them:*	Matthew 6:7-8 But **when ye pray, use not vain repetitions, as the heathen do: for they think that they shall be heard for their much speaking. Be not ye therefore like unto them:** for your Father knoweth what things ye have need of, before ye ask him.

Number	Commandment	Context of Commandment
31	*After this manner therefore pray ye: Our Father which art in heaven, Hallowed be thy name. Thy kingdom come, Thy will be done in earth, as it is in heaven. Give us this day our daily bread. And forgive us our debts, as we forgive our debtors. And lead us not into temptation, but deliver us from evil: For thine is the kingdom, and the power, and the glory, for ever. Amen.*	Matthew 6:9-13 **After this manner therefore pray ye: Our Father which art in heaven, Hallowed be thy name. Thy kingdom come,** Thy will be done in earth, as it is in heaven. Give us this day our daily bread. And forgive us our debts, as we forgive our debtors. And lead us not into temptation, but deliver us from evil: For thine is the kingdom, and the power, and the glory, for ever. Amen.
32	*when ye fast, be not, as the hypocrites, of a sad countenance:*	Matthew 6:16 Moreover **when ye fast, be not, as the hypocrites, of a sad countenance:** for they disfigure their faces, that they may appear unto men to fast. Verily I say unto you, They have their reward.
33	*when thou fastest, anoint thine head, and wash thy face;*	Matthew 6:17-18 But thou, **when thou fastest, anoint thine head, and wash thy face;** That thou appear not unto men to fast, but unto thy Father which is in secret: and thy Father, which seeth in secret, shall reward thee openly.

Number	Commandment	Context of Commandment
34	*Lay not up for yourselves treasures upon earth, where moth and rust doth corrupt, and where thieves break through and steal:*	Matthew 6:19 **Lay not up for yourselves treasures upon earth, where moth and rust doth corrupt, and where thieves break through and steal:**
35	*lay up for yourselves treasures in heaven, where neither moth nor rust doth corrupt, and where thieves do not break through nor steal:*	Matthew 6:20-21 But **lay up for yourselves treasures in heaven, where neither moth nor rust doth corrupt, and where thieves do not break through nor steal:** For where your treasure is, there will your heart be also.
36	*Take no thought for your life, what ye shall eat, or what ye shall drink; nor yet for your body, what ye shall put on.*	Matthew 6:24-25 No man can serve two masters: for either he will hate the one, and love the other; or else he will hold to the one, and despise the other. Ye cannot serve God and mammon. Therefore I say unto you, **Take no thought for your life, what ye shall eat, or what ye shall drink; nor yet for your body, what ye shall put on.** Is not the life more than meat, and the body than raiment?
37	*Behold the fowls of the air: for they sow not, neither do they reap, nor gather into barns; yet your heavenly Father feedeth them.*	Matthew 6:26 **Behold the fowls of the air: for they sow not, neither do they reap, nor gather into barns; yet your heavenly Father feedeth them.** Are ye not much better than they?

Number	Commandment	Context of Commandment
38	*Consider the lilies of the field, how they grow; they toil not, neither do they spin: And yet I say unto you, That even Solomon in all his glory was not arrayed like one of these.*	Matthew 6:27-29 Which of you by taking thought can add one cubit unto his stature? And why take ye thought for raiment? **Consider the lilies of the field, how they grow; they toil not, neither do they spin: And yet I say unto you, That even Solomon in all his glory was not arrayed like one of these.**
39	*take no thought, saying, What shall we eat? or, What shall we drink? or, Wherewithal shall we be clothed?*	Matthew 6:30-32 Wherefore, if God so clothe the grass of the field, which to day is, and to morrow is cast into the oven, shall he not much more clothe you, O ye of little faith? Therefore **take no thought, saying, What shall we eat? or, What shall we drink? or, Wherewithal shall we be clothed?** (For after all these things do the Gentiles seek:) for your heavenly Father knoweth that ye have need of all these things.
40	*seek ye first the kingdom of God, and his righteousness;*	Matthew 6:33 But **seek ye first the kingdom of God, and his righteousness;** and all these things shall be added unto you.
41	*Take therefore no thought for the morrow:*	Matthew 6:34 **Take therefore no thought for the morrow:** for the morrow shall take thought for the things of itself. Sufficient unto the day is the evil thereof.
42	*Judge not, that ye be not judged.*	Matthew 7:1-2 **Judge not, that ye be not judged.** For with what judgment ye judge, ye shall be judged: and with what measure ye mete, it shall be measured to you again.

Number	Commandment	Context of Commandment
43	*first cast out the beam out of thine own eye; and then shalt thou see clearly to cast out the mote out of thy brother's eye.*	Matthew 7:3-5 And why beholdest thou the mote that is in thy brother's eye, but considerest not the beam that is in thine own eye? Or how wilt thou say to thy brother, Let me pull out the mote out of thine eye; and, behold, a beam is in thine own eye? Thou hypocrite, **first cast out the beam out of thine own eye; and then shalt thou see clearly to cast out the mote out of thy brother's eye.**
44	*Give not that which is holy unto the dogs, neither cast ye your pearls before swine, lest they trample them under their feet, and turn again and rend you.*	Matthew 7:6 **Give not that which is holy unto the dogs, neither cast ye your pearls before swine, lest they trample them under their feet, and turn again and rend you.**
45	*Ask, and it shall be given you;*	Matthew 7:7 **Ask, and it shall be given you;** seek, and ye shall find; knock, and it shall be opened unto you:
46	*seek, and ye shall find;*	Matthew 7:7 Ask, and it shall be given you; **seek, and ye shall find;** knock, and it shall be opened unto you:

Number	Commandment	Context of Commandment
47	*knock, and it shall be opened unto you:*	Matthew 7:7-11 Ask, and it shall be given you; seek, and ye shall find; **knock, and it shall be opened unto you:** For every one that asketh receiveth; and he that seeketh findeth; and to him that knocketh it shall be opened. Or what man is there of you, whom if his son ask bread, will he give him a stone? Or if he ask a fish, will he give him a serpent? If ye then, being evil, know how to give good gifts unto your children, how much more shall your Father which is in heaven give good things to them that ask him?
48	*all things whatsoever ye would that men should do to you, do ye even so to them:*	Matthew 7:12 Therefore **all things whatsoever ye would that men should do to you, do ye even so to them:** for this is the law and the prophets.
49	*Enter ye in at the strait gate:*	Matthew 7:13-14 **Enter ye in at the strait gate:** for wide is the gate, and broad is the way, that leadeth to destruction, and many there be which go in thereat: Because strait is the gate, and narrow is the way, which leadeth unto life, and few there be that find it.

Number	Commandment	Context of Commandment
50	*Beware of false prophets, which come to you in sheep's clothing, but inwardly they are ravening wolves.*	Matthew 7:15-23 **Beware of false prophets, which come to you in sheep's clothing, but inwardly they are ravening wolves.** Ye shall know them by their fruits. Do men gather grapes of thorns, or figs of thistles? Even so every good tree bringeth forth good fruit; but a corrupt tree bringeth forth evil fruit. A good tree cannot bring forth evil fruit, neither can a corrupt tree bring forth good fruit. Every tree that bringeth not forth good fruit is hewn down, and cast into the fire. Wherefore by their fruits ye shall know them. Not every one that saith unto me, Lord, Lord, shall enter into the kingdom of heaven; but he that doeth the will of my Father which is in heaven. Many will say to me in that day, Lord, Lord, have we not prophesied in thy name? and in thy name have cast out devils? and in thy name done many wonderful works? And then will I profess unto them, I never knew you: depart from me, ye that work iniquity.
51	*be thou clean.*	Matthew 8:1-3 When he was come down from the mountain, great multitudes followed him. And, behold, there came a leper and worshipped him, saying, Lord, if thou wilt, thou canst make me clean. And Jesus put forth his hand, and touched him, saying, I will; **be thou clean.** And immediately his leprosy was cleansed.
52	*See thou tell no man; but go thy way, shew thyself to the priest, and offer the gift that Moses commanded, for a testimony unto them.*	Matthew 8:4 And Jesus saith unto him, **See thou tell no man; but go thy way, shew thyself to the priest, and offer the gift that Moses commanded, for a testimony unto them.**

Number	Commandment	Context of Commandment
53	*Go thy way; and as thou hast believed, so be it done unto thee.*	Matthew 8:5-13 And when Jesus was entered into Capernaum, there came unto him a centurion, beseeching him, And saying, Lord, my servant lieth at home sick of the palsy, grievously tormented. And Jesus saith unto him, I will come and heal him. The centurion answered and said, Lord, I am not worthy that thou shouldest come under my roof: but speak the word only, and my servant shall be healed. For I am a man under authority, having soldiers under me: and I say to this man, Go, and he goeth; and to another, Come, and he cometh; and to my servant, Do this, and he doeth it. When Jesus heard it, he marvelled, and said to them that followed, Verily I say unto you, I have not found so great faith, no, not in Israel. And I say unto you, That many shall come from the east and west, and shall sit down with Abraham, and Isaac, and Jacob, in the kingdom of heaven. But the children of the kingdom shall be cast out into outer darkness: there shall be weeping and gnashing of teeth. And Jesus said unto the centurion, **Go thy way; and as thou hast believed, so be it done unto thee.** And his servant was healed in the selfsame hour.
54	*Go.*	Matthew 8:28-32 And when he was come to the other side into the country of the Gergesenes, there met him two possessed with devils, coming out of the tombs, exceeding fierce, so that no man might pass by that way. And, behold, they cried out, saying, What have we to do with thee, Jesus, thou Son of God? art thou come hither to torment us before the time? And there was a good way off from them an herd of many swine feeding. So the devils besought him, saying, If thou cast us out, suffer us to go away into the herd of swine. And he said unto them, **Go.** And when they were come out, they went into the herd of swine: and, behold, the whole herd of swine ran violently down a steep place into the sea, and perished in the waters.

Number	Commandment	Context of Commandment
55	*be of good cheer; thy sins be forgiven thee.*	Matthew 9:1-2 And he entered into a ship, and passed over, and came into his own city. And, behold, they brought to him a man sick of the palsy, lying on a bed: and Jesus seeing their faith said unto the sick of the palsy; Son, **be of good cheer; thy sins be forgiven thee.**
56	*Arise, take up thy bed, and go unto thine house.*	Matthew 9:3-7 And, behold, certain of the scribes said within themselves, This man blasphemeth. And Jesus knowing their thoughts said, Wherefore think ye evil in your hearts? For whether is easier, to say, Thy sins be forgiven thee; or to say, Arise, and walk? But that ye may know that the Son of man hath power on earth to forgive sins, (then saith he to the sick of the palsy,) **Arise, take up thy bed, and go unto thine house.** And he arose, and departed to his house.
57	*Follow me.*	Matthew 9:9 And as Jesus passed forth from thence, he saw a man, named Matthew, sitting at the receipt of custom: and he saith unto him, **Follow me.** And he arose, and followed him.
58	*go ye and learn what that meaneth, I will have mercy, and not sacrifice:*	Matthew 9:11-13 And when the Pharisees saw it, they said unto his disciples, Why eateth your Master with publicans and sinners? But when Jesus heard that, he said unto them, They that be whole need not a physician, but they that are sick. But **go ye and learn what that meaneth, I will have mercy, and not sacrifice:** for I am not come to call the righteous, but sinners to repentance.
59	*Give place:*	Matthew 9:23-25 And when Jesus came into the ruler's house, and saw the minstrels and the people making a noise, He said unto them, **Give place:** for the maid is not dead, but sleepeth. And they laughed him to scorn. But when the people were put forth, he went in, and took her by the hand, and the maid arose.

Number	Commandment	Context of Commandment
60	*According to your faith be it unto you.*	Matthew 9:27-29 And when Jesus departed thence, two blind men followed him, crying, and saying, Thou son of David, have mercy on us. And when he was come into the house, the blind men came to him: and Jesus saith unto them, Believe ye that I am able to do this? They said unto him, Yea, Lord. Then touched he their eyes, saying, **According to your faith be it unto you.**
61	*See that no man know it.*	Matthew 9:30-31 And their eyes were opened; and Jesus straitly charged them, saying, **See that no man know it.** But they, when they were departed, spread abroad his fame in all that country.
62	*Pray ye therefore the Lord of the harvest, that he will send forth labourers into his harvest.*	Matthew 9:35-38 And Jesus went about all the cities and villages, teaching in their synagogues, and preaching the gospel of the kingdom, and healing every sickness and every disease among the people. But when he saw the multitudes, he was moved with compassion on them, because they fainted, and were scattered abroad, as sheep having no shepherd. Then saith he unto his disciples, The harvest truly is plenteous, but the labourers are few; **Pray ye therefore the Lord of the harvest, that he will send forth labourers into his harvest.**

Number	Commandment	Context of Commandment
63	*Go not into the way of the Gentiles, and into any city of the Samaritans enter ye not: But go rather to the lost sheep of the house of Israel.*	Matthew 10:1-6 And when he had called unto him his twelve disciples, he gave them power against unclean spirits, to cast them out, and to heal all manner of sickness and all manner of disease. Now the names of the twelve apostles are these; The first, Simon, who is called Peter, and Andrew his brother; James the son of Zebedee, and John his brother; Philip, and Bartholomew; Thomas, and Matthew the publican; James the son of Alphaeus, and Lebbaeus, whose surname was Thaddaeus; Simon the Canaanite, and Judas Iscariot, who also betrayed him. These twelve Jesus sent forth, and commanded them, saying, **Go not into the way of the Gentiles, and into any city of the Samaritans enter ye not: But go rather to the lost sheep of the house of Israel.**
64	*as ye go, preach, saying, The kingdom of heaven is at hand.*	Matthew 10:7 And **as ye go, preach, saying, The kingdom of heaven is at hand.**
65	*Heal the sick,*	Matthew 10:8 **Heal the sick,** cleanse the lepers, raise the dead, cast out devils: freely ye have received, freely give.
66	*cleanse the lepers,*	Matthew 10:8 Heal the sick, **cleanse the lepers,** raise the dead, cast out devils: freely ye have received, freely give.
67	*raise the dead,*	Matthew 10:8 Heal the sick, cleanse the lepers, **raise the dead,** cast out devils: freely ye have received, freely give.

Number	Commandment	Context of Commandment
68	*cast out devils:*	Matthew 10:8 Heal the sick, cleanse the lepers, raise the dead, **cast out devils:** freely ye have received, freely give.
69	*freely ye have received, freely give.*	Matthew 10:8 Heal the sick, cleanse the lepers, raise the dead, cast out devils: **freely ye have received, freely give.**
70	*Provide neither gold, nor silver, nor brass in your purses, Nor scrip for your journey, neither two coats, neither shoes, nor yet staves:*	Matthew 10:9-10 **Provide neither gold, nor silver, nor brass in your purses, Nor scrip for your journey, neither two coats, neither shoes, nor yet staves:** for the workman is worthy of his meat.
71	*into whatsoever city or town ye shall enter, enquire who in it is worthy; and there abide till ye go thence.*	Matthew 10:11 And **into whatsoever city or town ye shall enter, enquire who in it is worthy; and there abide till ye go thence.**
72	*when ye come into an house, salute it. And if the house be worthy, let your peace come upon it: but if it be not worthy, let your peace return to you.*	Matthew 10:12-13 And **when ye come into an house, salute it. And if the house be worthy, let your peace come upon it: but if it be not worthy, let your peace return to you.**

Number	Commandment	Context of Commandment
73	*whosoever shall not receive you, nor hear your words, when ye depart out of that house or city, shake off the dust of your feet.*	Matthew 10:14-15 And **whosoever shall not receive you, nor hear your words, when ye depart out of that house or city, shake off the dust of your feet.** Verily I say unto you, It shall be more tolerable for the land of Sodom and Gomorrha in the day of judgment, than for that city.
74	*Behold, I send you forth as sheep in the midst of wolves:*	Matthew 10:16 **Behold, I send you forth as sheep in the midst of wolves:** be ye therefore wise as serpents, and harmless as doves.
75	*be ye therefore wise as serpents, and harmless as doves.*	Matthew 10:16 Behold, I send you forth as sheep in the midst of wolves: **be ye therefore wise as serpents, and harmless as doves.**
76	*beware of men:*	Matthew 10:17-18 But **beware of men:** for they will deliver you up to the councils, and they will scourge you in their synagogues; And ye shall be brought before governors and kings for my sake, for a testimony against them and the Gentiles.
77	*But when they deliver you up, take no thought how or what ye shall speak: for it shall be given you in that same hour what ye shall speak.*	Matthew 10:19-20 **But when they deliver you up, take no thought how or what ye shall speak: for it shall be given you in that same hour what ye shall speak.** For it is not ye that speak, but the Spirit of your Father which speaketh in you.

Number	Commandment	Context of Commandment
78	*when they persecute you in this city, flee ye into another:*	Matthew 10:21-23 And the brother shall deliver up the brother to death, and the father the child: and the children shall rise up against their parents, and cause them to be put to death. And ye shall be hated of all men for my name's sake: but he that endureth to the end shall be saved. But **when they persecute you in this city, flee ye into another:** for verily I say unto you, Ye shall not have gone over the cities of Israel, till the Son of man be come.
79	*Fear them not therefore: for there is nothing covered, that shall not be revealed; and hid, that shall not be known.*	Matthew 10:24-26 The disciple is not above his master, nor the servant above his lord. It is enough for the disciple that he be as his master, and the servant as his lord. If they have called the master of the house Beelzebub, how much more shall they call them of his household? **Fear them not therefore: for there is nothing covered, that shall not be revealed; and hid, that shall not be known.**
80	*What I tell you in darkness, that speak ye in light:*	Matthew 10:27 **What I tell you in darkness, that speak ye in light:** and what ye hear in the ear, that preach ye upon the housetops.
81	*what ye hear in the ear, that preach ye upon the housetops.*	Matthew 10:27 What I tell you in darkness, that speak ye in light: and **what ye hear in the ear, that preach ye upon the housetops.**
82	*fear not them which kill the body, but are not able to kill the soul:*	Matthew 10:28 And **fear not them which kill the body, but are not able to kill the soul:** but rather fear him which is able to destroy both soul and body in hell.

Number	Commandment	Context of Commandment
83	*fear him which is able to destroy both soul and body in hell.*	Matthew 10:28 And fear not them which kill the body, but are not able to kill the soul: but rather **fear him which is able to destroy both soul and body in hell.**
84	*Fear ye not therefore, ye are of more value than many sparrows.*	Matthew 10:29-31 Are not two sparrows sold for a farthing? and one of them shall not fall on the ground without your Father. But the very hairs of your head are all numbered. **Fear ye not therefore, ye are of more value than many sparrows.**
85	*Think not that I am come to send peace on earth:*	Matthew 10:32-36 Whosoever therefore shall confess me before men, him will I confess also before my Father which is in heaven. But whosoever shall deny me before men, him will I also deny before my Father which is in heaven. **Think not that I am come to send peace on earth:** I came not to send peace, but a sword. For I am come to set a man at variance against his father, and the daughter against her mother, and the daughter in law against her mother in law. And a man's foes shall be they of his own household.
86	*Go and shew John again those things which ye do hear and see: The blind receive their sight, and the lame walk, the lepers are cleansed, and the deaf hear, the dead are raised up, and the poor have the gospel preached to them. And blessed is he, whosoever shall not be offended in me.*	Matthew 11:2-6 Now when John had heard in the prison the works of Christ, he sent two of his disciples, And said unto him, Art thou he that should come, or do we look for another? Jesus answered and said unto them, **Go and shew John again those things which ye do hear and see: The blind receive their sight, and the lame walk, the lepers are cleansed, and the deaf hear, the dead are raised up, and the poor have the gospel preached to them. And blessed is he, whosoever shall not be offended in me.**

Commandments of Jesus Christ found in: The Gospel According To Matthew

Number	Commandment	Context of Commandment
87	*He that hath ears to hear, let him hear.*	Matthew 11:13-15 For all the prophets and the law prophesied until John. And if ye will receive it, this is Elias, which was for to come. **He that hath ears to hear, let him hear.**
88	*Come unto me, all ye that labour and are heavy laden, and I will give you rest.*	Matthew 11:27-28 All things are delivered unto me of my Father: and no man knoweth the Son, but the Father; neither knoweth any man the Father, save the Son, and he to whomsoever the Son will reveal him. **Come unto me, all ye that labour and are heavy laden, and I will give you rest.**
89	*Take my yoke upon you, and learn of me;*	Matthew 11:29-30 **Take my yoke upon you, and learn of me;** for I am meek and lowly in heart: and ye shall find rest unto your souls. For my yoke is easy, and my burden is light.
90	*Either make the tree good, and his fruit good; or else make the tree corrupt, and his fruit corrupt:*	Matthew 12:33 **Either make the tree good, and his fruit good; or else make the tree corrupt, and his fruit corrupt:** for the tree is known by his fruit.

Number	Commandment	Context of Commandment
91	*Behold my mother and my brethren!*	Matthew 12:46-50 While he yet talked to the people, behold, his mother and his brethren stood without, desiring to speak with him. Then one said unto him, Behold, thy mother and thy brethren stand without, desiring to speak with thee. But he answered and said unto him that told him, Who is my mother? and who are my brethren? And he stretched forth his hand toward his disciples, and said, **Behold my mother and my brethren!** For whosoever shall do the will of my Father which is in heaven, the same is my brother, and sister, and mother.
92	*Behold, a sower went forth to sow;*	Matthew 13:3-9 And he spake many things unto them in parables, saying, **Behold, a sower went forth to sow;** And when he sowed, some seeds fell by the way side, and the fowls came and devoured them up: Some fell upon stony places, where they had not much earth: and forthwith they sprung up, because they had no deepness of earth: And when the sun was up, they were scorched; and because they had no root, they withered away. And some fell among thorns; and the thorns sprung up, and choked them: But other fell into good ground, and brought forth fruit, some an hundredfold, some sixtyfold, some thirtyfold. Who hath ears to hear, let him hear.
93	*Who hath ears to hear, let him hear.*	Matthew 13:9 **Who hath ears to hear, let him hear.**

Number	Commandment	Context of Commandment
94	*Hear ye therefore the parable of the sower.*	Matthew 13:17-23 For verily I say unto you, That many prophets and righteous men have desired to see those things which ye see, and have not seen them; and to hear those things which ye hear, and have not heard them. **Hear ye therefore the parable of the sower.** When any one heareth the word of the kingdom, and understandeth it not, then cometh the wicked one, and catcheth away that which was sown in his heart. This is he which received seed by the way side. But he that received the seed into stony places, the same is he that heareth the word, and anon with joy receiveth it; Yet hath he not root in himself, but dureth for a while: for when tribulation or persecution ariseth because of the word, by and by he is offended. He also that received seed among the thorns is he that heareth the word; and the care of this world, and the deceitfulness of riches, choke the word, and he becometh unfruitful. But he that received seed into the good ground is he that heareth the word, and understandeth it; which also beareth fruit, and bringeth forth, some an hundredfold, some sixty, some thirty.
95	*Who hath ears to hear, let him hear.*	Matthew 13:36-43 Then Jesus sent the multitude away, and went into the house: and his disciples came unto him, saying, Declare unto us the parable of the tares of the field. He answered and said unto them, He that soweth the good seed is the Son of man; The field is the world; the good seed are the children of the kingdom; but the tares are the children of the wicked one; The enemy that sowed them is the devil; the harvest is the end of the world; and the reapers are the angels. As therefore the tares are gathered and burned in the fire; so shall it be in the end of this world. The Son of man shall send forth his angels, and they shall gather out of his kingdom all things that offend, and them which do iniquity; And shall cast them into a furnace of fire: there shall be wailing and gnashing of teeth. Then shall the righteous shine forth as the sun in the kingdom of their Father. **Who hath ears to hear, let him hear.**

Number	Commandment	Context of Commandment
96	*give ye them to eat.*	Matthew 14:14-16 And Jesus went forth, and saw a great multitude, and was moved with compassion toward them, and he healed their sick. And when it was evening, his disciples came to him, saying, This is a desert place, and the time is now past; send the multitude away, that they may go into the villages, and buy themselves victuals. But Jesus said unto them, They need not depart; **give ye them to eat.**
97	*Bring them hither to me.*	Matthew 14:17-20 And they say unto him, We have here but five loaves, and two fishes. He said, **Bring them hither to me.** And he commanded the multitude to sit down on the grass, and took the five loaves, and the two fishes, and looking up to heaven, he blessed, and brake, and gave the loaves to his disciples, and the disciples to the multitude. And they did all eat, and were filled: and they took up of the fragments that remained twelve baskets full.
98	*Be of good cheer; it is I; be not afraid.*	Matthew 14:23-27 And when he had sent the multitudes away, he went up into a mountain apart to pray: and when the evening was come, he was there alone. But the ship was now in the midst of the sea, tossed with waves: for the wind was contrary. And in the fourth watch of the night Jesus went unto them, walking on the sea. And when the disciples saw him walking on the sea, they were troubled, saying, It is a spirit; and they cried out for fear. But straightway Jesus spake unto them, saying, **Be of good cheer; it is I; be not afraid.**

Number	Commandment	Context of Commandment
99	*Come.*	Matthew 14:28-33 And Peter answered him and said, Lord, if it be thou, bid me come unto thee on the water. And he said, **Come.** And when Peter was come down out of the ship, he walked on the water, to go to Jesus. But when he saw the wind boisterous, he was afraid; and beginning to sink, he cried, saying, Lord, save me. And immediately Jesus stretched forth his hand, and caught him, and said unto him, O thou of little faith, wherefore didst thou doubt? And when they were come into the ship, the wind ceased. Then they that were in the ship came and worshipped him, saying, Of a truth thou art the Son of God.
100	*Hear, and understand: Not that which goeth into the mouth defileth a man; but that which cometh out of the mouth, this defileth a man.*	Matthew 15:1-11 Then came to Jesus scribes and Pharisees, which were of Jerusalem, saying, Why do thy disciples transgress the tradition of the elders? for they wash not their hands when they eat bread. But he answered and said unto them, Why do ye also transgress the commandment of God by your tradition? For God commanded, saying, Honour thy father and mother: and, He that curseth father or mother, let him die the death. But ye say, Whosoever shall say to his father or his mother, It is a gift, by whatsoever thou mightest be profited by me; And honour not his father or his mother, he shall be free. Thus have ye made the commandment of God of none effect by your tradition. Ye hypocrites, well did Esaias prophesy of you, saying, This people draweth nigh unto me with their mouth, and honoureth me with their lips; but their heart is far from me. But in vain they do worship me, teaching for doctrines the commandments of men. And he called the multitude, and said unto them, **Hear, and understand: Not that which goeth into the mouth defileth a man; but that which cometh out of the mouth, this defileth a man.**

Number	Commandment	Context of Commandment
101	*Let them alone:*	Matthew 15:12-14 Then came his disciples, and said unto him, Knowest thou that the Pharisees were offended, after they heard this saying? But he answered and said, Every plant, which my heavenly Father hath not planted, shall be rooted up. **Let them alone:** they be blind leaders of the blind. And if the blind lead the blind, both shall fall into the ditch.
102	*be it unto thee even as thou wilt.*	Matthew 15:21-28 Then Jesus went thence, and departed into the coasts of Tyre and Sidon. And, behold, a woman of Canaan came out of the same coasts, and cried unto him, saying, Have mercy on me, O Lord, thou son of David; my daughter is grievously vexed with a devil. But he answered her not a word. And his disciples came and besought him, saying, Send her away; for she crieth after us. But he answered and said, I am not sent but unto the lost sheep of the house of Israel. Then came she and worshipped him, saying, Lord, help me. But he answered and said, It is not meet to take the children's bread, and to cast it to dogs. And she said, Truth, Lord: yet the dogs eat of the crumbs which fall from their masters' table. Then Jesus answered and said unto her, O woman, great is thy faith: **be it unto thee even as thou wilt.** And her daughter was made whole from that very hour.

Number	Commandment	Context of Commandment
103	*Take heed and beware of the leaven of the Pharisees and of the Sadducees.*	Matthew 16:6-12 Then Jesus said unto them, **Take heed and beware of the leaven of the Pharisees and of the Sadducees.** And they reasoned among themselves, saying, It is because we have taken no bread. Which when Jesus perceived, he said unto them, O ye of little faith, why reason ye among yourselves, because ye have brought no bread? Do ye not yet understand, neither remember the five loaves of the five thousand, and how many baskets ye took up? Neither the seven loaves of the four thousand, and how many baskets ye took up? How is it that ye do not understand that I spake it not to you concerning bread, that ye should beware of the leaven of the Pharisees and of the Sadducees? Then understood they how that he bade them not beware of the leaven of bread, but of the doctrine of the Pharisees and of the Sadducees.
104	*Get thee behind me, Satan: thou art an offence unto me: for thou savourest not the things that be of God, but those that be of men.*	Matthew 16:21-23 From that time forth began Jesus to shew unto his disciples, how that he must go unto Jerusalem, and suffer many things of the elders and chief priests and scribes, and be killed, and be raised again the third day. Then Peter took him, and began to rebuke him, saying, Be it far from thee, Lord: this shall not be unto thee. But he turned, and said unto Peter, **Get thee behind me, Satan: thou art an offence unto me: for thou savourest not the things that be of God, but those that be of men.**
105	*If any man will come after me, let him deny himself, and take up his cross, and follow me.*	Matthew 16:24-26 Then said Jesus unto his disciples, **If any man will come after me, let him deny himself, and take up his cross, and follow me.** For whosoever will save his life shall lose it: and whosoever will lose his life for my sake shall find it. For what is a man profited, if he shall gain the whole world, and lose his own soul? or what shall a man give in exchange for his soul?

Number	Commandment	Context of Commandment
106	*Arise, and be not afraid.*	Matthew 17:1-8 And after six days Jesus taketh Peter, James, and John his brother, and bringeth them up into an high mountain apart, And was transfigured before them: and his face did shine as the sun, and his raiment was white as the light. And, behold, there appeared unto them Moses and Elias talking with him. Then answered Peter, and said unto Jesus, Lord, it is good for us to be here: if thou wilt, let us make here three tabernacles; one for thee, and one for Moses, and one for Elias. While he yet spake, behold, a bright cloud overshadowed them: and behold a voice out of the cloud, which said, This is my beloved Son, in whom I am well pleased; hear ye him. And when the disciples heard it, they fell on their face, and were sore afraid. And Jesus came and touched them, and said, **Arise, and be not afraid.** And when they had lifted up their eyes, they saw no man, save Jesus only.
107	*Tell the vision to no man, until the Son of man be risen again from the dead.*	Matthew 17:9 And as they came down from the mountain, Jesus charged them, saying, **Tell the vision to no man, until the Son of man be risen again from the dead.**
108	*go thou to the sea, and cast an hook, and take up the fish that first cometh up; and when thou hast opened his mouth, thou shalt find a piece of money: that take, and give unto them for me and thee.*	Matthew 17:24-27 And when they were come to Capernaum, they that received tribute money came to Peter, and said, Doth not your master pay tribute? He saith, Yes. And when he was come into the house, Jesus prevented him, saying, What thinkest thou, Simon? of whom do the kings of the earth take custom or tribute? of their own children, or of strangers? Peter saith unto him, Of strangers. Jesus saith unto him, Then are the children free. Notwithstanding, lest we should offend them, **go thou to the sea, and cast an hook, and take up the fish that first cometh up; and when thou hast opened his mouth, thou shalt find a piece of money: that take, and give unto them for me and thee.**

Commandments of Jesus Christ found in: The Gospel According To Matthew

Number	Commandment	Context of Commandment
109	*if thy hand or thy foot offend thee, cut them off, and cast them from thee:*	Matthew 18:8 Wherefore **if thy hand or thy foot offend thee, cut them off, and cast them from thee:** it is better for thee to enter into life halt or maimed, rather than having two hands or two feet to be cast into everlasting fire.
110	*if thine eye offend thee, pluck it out, and cast it from thee:*	Matthew 18:9 And **if thine eye offend thee, pluck it out, and cast it from thee:** it is better for thee to enter into life with one eye, rather than having two eyes to be cast into hell fire.
111	*Take heed that ye despise not one of these little ones;*	Matthew 18:4-10 Whosoever therefore shall humble himself as this little child, the same is greatest in the kingdom of heaven. And whoso shall receive one such little child in my name receiveth me. But whoso shall offend one of these little ones which believe in me, it were better for him that a millstone were hanged about his neck, and that he were drowned in the depth of the sea. Woe unto the world because of offences! for it must needs be that offences come; but woe to that man by whom the offence cometh! Wherefore if thy hand or thy foot offend thee, cut them off, and cast them from thee: it is better for thee to enter into life halt or maimed, rather than having two hands or two feet to be cast into everlasting fire. And if thine eye offend thee, pluck it out, and cast it from thee: it is better for thee to enter into life with one eye, rather than having two eyes to be cast into hell fire. **Take heed that ye despise not one of these little ones;** for I say unto you, That in heaven their angels do always behold the face of my Father which is in heaven.

Number	Commandment	Context of Commandment
112	*if thy brother shall trespass against thee, go and tell him his fault between thee and him alone:*	Matthew 18:15 Moreover **if thy brother shall trespass against thee, go and tell him his fault between thee and him alone:** if he shall hear thee, thou hast gained thy brother.
113	*if he will not hear thee, then take with thee one or two more, that in the mouth of two or three witnesses every word may be established.*	Matthew 18:16 But **if he will not hear thee, then take with thee one or two more, that in the mouth of two or three witnesses every word may be established.**
114	*if he shall neglect to hear them, tell it unto the church:*	Matthew 18:17 And **if he shall neglect to hear them, tell it unto the church:** but if he neglect to hear the church, let him be unto thee as an heathen man and a publican.
115	*if he neglect to hear the church, let him be unto thee as an heathen man and a publican.*	Matthew 18:17 And if he shall neglect to hear them, tell it unto the church: but **if he neglect to hear the church, let him be unto thee as an heathen man and a publican.**
116	*What therefore God hath joined together, let not man put asunder.*	Matthew 19:3-6 The Pharisees also came unto him, tempting him, and saying unto him, Is it lawful for a man to put away his wife for every cause? And he answered and said unto them, Have ye not read, that he which made them at the beginning made them male and female, And said, For this cause shall a man leave father and mother, and shall cleave to his wife: and they twain shall be one flesh? Wherefore they are no more twain, but one flesh. **What therefore God hath joined together, let not man put asunder.**

34

Number	Commandment	Context of Commandment
117	*He that is able to receive it, let him receive it.*	Matthew 19:7-12 They say unto him, Why did Moses then command to give a writing of divorcement, and to put her away? He saith unto them, Moses because of the hardness of your hearts suffered you to put away your wives: but from the beginning it was not so. And I say unto you, Whosoever shall put away his wife, except it be for fornication, and shall marry another, committeth adultery: and whoso marrieth her which is put away doth commit adultery. His disciples say unto him, If the case of the man be so with his wife, it is not good to marry. But he said unto them, All men cannot receive this saying, save they to whom it is given. For there are some eunuchs, which were so born from their mother's womb: and there are some eunuchs, which were made eunuchs of men: and there be eunuchs, which have made themselves eunuchs for the kingdom of heaven's sake. **He that is able to receive it, let him receive it.**
118	*Suffer little children, and forbid them not, to come unto me:*	Matthew 19:13-14 Then were there brought unto him little children, that he should put his hands on them, and pray: and the disciples rebuked them. But Jesus said, **Suffer little children, and forbid them not, to come unto me:** for of such is the kingdom of heaven.
119	*if thou wilt enter into life, keep the commandments.*	Matthew 19:16-20 And, behold, one came and said unto him, Good Master, what good thing shall I do, that I may have eternal life? And he said unto him, Why callest thou me good? there is none good but one, that is, God: but **if thou wilt enter into life, keep the commandments.** He saith unto him, Which? Jesus said, Thou shalt do no murder, Thou shalt not commit adultery, Thou shalt not steal, Thou shalt not bear false witness, Honour thy father and thy mother: and, Thou shalt love thy neighbour as thyself. The young man saith unto him, All these things have I kept from my youth up: what lack I yet?

Number	Commandment	Context of Commandment
120	*If thou wilt be perfect, go and sell that thou hast, and give to the poor, and thou shalt have treasure in heaven: and come and follow me.*	**Matthew 19:20-22** The young man saith unto him, All these things have I kept from my youth up: what lack I yet? Jesus said unto him, **If thou wilt be perfect, go and sell that thou hast, and give to the poor, and thou shalt have treasure in heaven: and come and follow me.** But when the young man heard that saying, he went away sorrowful: for he had great possessions.
121	*Behold, we go up to Jerusalem; and the Son of man shall be betrayed unto the chief priests and unto the scribes, and they shall condemn him to death, And shall deliver him to the Gentiles to mock, and to scourge, and to crucify him: and the third day he shall rise again.*	**Matthew 20:18-19** **Behold, we go up to Jerusalem; and the Son of man shall be betrayed unto the chief priests and unto the scribes, and they shall condemn him to death, And shall deliver him to the Gentiles to mock, and to scourge, and to crucify him: and the third day he shall rise again.**

Number	Commandment	Context of Commandment
122	*whosoever will be great among you, let him be your minister;*	Matthew 20:20-26 Then came to him the mother of Zebedees children with her sons, worshipping him, and desiring a certain thing of him. And he said unto her, What wilt thou? She saith unto him, Grant that these my two sons may sit, the one on thy right hand, and the other on the left, in thy kingdom. But Jesus answered and said, Ye know not what ye ask. Are ye able to drink of the cup that I shall drink of, and to be baptized with the baptism that I am baptized with? They say unto him, We are able. And he saith unto them, Ye shall drink indeed of my cup, and be baptized with the baptism that I am baptized with: but to sit on my right hand, and on my left, is not mine to give, but it shall be given to them for whom it is prepared of my Father. And when the ten heard it, they were moved with indignation against the two brethren. But Jesus called them unto him, and said, Ye know that the princes of the Gentiles exercise dominion over them, and they that are great exercise authority upon them. But it shall not be so among you: but **whosoever will be great among you, let him be your minister;**
123	*whosoever will be chief among you, let him be your servant:*	Matthew 20:27-28 And **whosoever will be chief among you, let him be your servant:** Even as the Son of man came not to be ministered unto, but to minister, and to give his life a ransom for many.
124	*Go into the village over against you, and straightway ye shall find an ass tied, and a colt with her:*	Matthew 21:1-2 And when they drew nigh unto Jerusalem, and were come to Bethphage, unto the mount of Olives, then sent Jesus two disciples, Saying unto them, **Go into the village over against you, and straightway ye shall find an ass tied, and a colt with her:** loose them, and bring them unto me.

Number	Commandment	Context of Commandment
125	*loose them,*	Matthew 21:2 Saying unto them, Go into the village over against you, and straightway ye shall find an ass tied, and a colt with her: **loose them,** and bring them unto me.
126	*bring them unto me.*	Matthew 21:2 Saying unto them, Go into the village over against you, and straightway ye shall find an ass tied, and a colt with her: loose them, and **bring them unto me.**
127	*if any man say ought unto you, ye shall say, The Lord hath need of them;*	Matthew 21:3 And **if any man say ought unto you, ye shall say, The Lord hath need of them;** and straightway he will send them.
128	*Let no fruit grow on thee henceforward for ever.*	Matthew 21:18-22 Now in the morning as he returned into the city, he hungered. And when he saw a fig tree in the way, he came to it, and found nothing thereon, but leaves only, and said unto it, **Let no fruit grow on thee henceforward for ever.** And presently the fig tree withered away. And when the disciples saw it, they marvelled, saying, How soon is the fig tree withered away! Jesus answered and said unto them, Verily I say unto you, If ye have faith, and doubt not, ye shall not only do this which is done to the fig tree, but also if ye shall say unto this mountain, Be thou removed, and be thou cast into the sea; it shall be done. And all things, whatsoever ye shall ask in prayer, believing, ye shall receive.

Number	Commandment	Context of Commandment
129	*Hear another parable:*	Matthew 21:33-39 **Hear another parable:** There was a certain householder, which planted a vineyard, and hedged it round about, and digged a winepress in it, and built a tower, and let it out to husbandmen, and went into a far country: And when the time of the fruit drew near, he sent his servants to the husbandmen, that they might receive the fruits of it. And the husbandmen took his servants, and beat one, and killed another, and stoned another. Again, he sent other servants more than the first: and they did unto them likewise. But last of all he sent unto them his son, saying, They will reverence my son. But when the husbandmen saw the son, they said among themselves, This is the heir; come, let us kill him, and let us seize on his inheritance. And they caught him, and cast him out of the vineyard, and slew him.
130	*Shew me the tribute money.*	Matthew 22:17-19 Tell us therefore, What thinkest thou? Is it lawful to give tribute unto Caesar, or not? But Jesus perceived their wickedness, and said, Why tempt ye me, ye hypocrites? **Shew me the tribute money.** And they brought unto him a penny.
131	*Render therefore unto Caesar the things which are Caesar's; and unto God the things that are God's.*	Matthew 22:20-21 And he saith unto them, Whose is this image and superscription? They say unto him, Caesar's. Then saith he unto them, **Render therefore unto Caesar the things which are Caesar's; and unto God the things that are God's.**

Number	Commandment	Context of Commandment
132	*All therefore whatsoever they bid you observe, that observe and do;*	Matthew 23:1-3 Then spake Jesus to the multitude, and to his disciples, Saying The scribes and the Pharisees sit in Moses' seat: **All therefore whatsoever they bid you observe, that observe and do;** but do not ye after their works: for they say, and do not.
133	*but do not ye after their works:*	Matthew 23:3-4 All therefore whatsoever they bid you observe, that observe and do; **but do not ye after their works:** for they say, and do not. For they bind heavy burdens and grievous to be borne, and lay them on men's shoulders; but they themselves will not move them with one of their fingers.
134	*be not ye called Rabbi:*	Matthew 23:5-8 But all their works they do for to be seen of men: they make broad their phylacteries, and enlarge the borders of their garments, And love the uppermost rooms at feasts, and the chief seats in the synagogues, And greetings in the markets, and to be called of men, Rabbi, Rabbi. But **be not ye called Rabbi:** for one is your Master, even Christ; and all ye are brethren.
135	*call no man your father upon the earth:*	Matthew 23:9 And **call no man your father upon the earth:** for one is your Father, which is in heaven.
136	*Neither be ye called masters:*	Matthew 23:10 **Neither be ye called masters:** for one is your Master, even Christ.
137	*cleanse first that which is within the cup and platter, that the outside of them may be clean also.*	Matthew 23:25-26 Woe unto you, scribes and Pharisees, hypocrites! for ye make clean the outside of the cup and of the platter, but within they are full of extortion and excess. Thou blind Pharisee, **cleanse first that which is within the cup and platter, that the outside of them may be clean also.**

Number	Commandment	Context of Commandment
138	*Fill ye up then the measure of your fathers.*	Matthew 23:29-32 Woe unto you, scribes and Pharisees, hypocrites! because ye build the tombs of the prophets, and garnish the sepulchres of the righteous, And say, If we had been in the days of our fathers, we would not have been partakers with them in the blood of the prophets. Wherefore ye be witnesses unto yourselves, that ye are the children of them which killed the prophets. **Fill ye up then the measure of your fathers.**
139	*behold, I send unto you prophets, and wise men, and scribes: and some of them ye shall kill and crucify; and some of them shall ye scourge in your synagogues, and persecute them from city to city: That upon you may come all the righteous blood shed upon the earth, from the blood of righteous Abel unto the blood of Zacharias son of Barachias, whom ye slew between the temple and the altar.*	Matthew 23:34-35 Wherefore, **behold, I send unto you prophets, and wise men, and scribes: and some of them ye shall kill and crucify; and some of them shall ye scourge in your synagogues, and persecute them from city to city: That upon you may come all the righteous blood shed upon the earth, from the blood of righteous Abel unto the blood of Zacharias son of Barachias, whom ye slew between the temple and the altar.**

Number	Commandment	Context of Commandment
140	*Behold, your house is left unto you desolate.*	Matthew 23:37-39 O Jerusalem, Jerusalem, thou that killest the prophets, and stonest them which are sent unto thee, how often would I have gathered thy children together, even as a hen gathereth her chickens under her wings, and ye would not! **Behold, your house is left unto you desolate.** For I say unto you, Ye shall not see me henceforth, till ye shall say, Blessed is he that cometh in the name of the Lord.
141	*Take heed that no man deceive you. For many shall come in my name, saying, I am Christ; and shall deceive many.*	Matthew 24:1-5 And Jesus went out, and departed from the temple: and his disciples came to him for to shew him the buildings of the temple. And Jesus said unto them, See ye not all these things? verily I say unto you, There shall not be left here one stone upon another, that shall not be thrown down. And as he sat upon the mount of Olives, the disciples came unto him privately, saying, Tell us, when shall these things be? and what shall be the sign of thy coming, and of the end of the world? And Jesus answered and said unto them, **Take heed that no man deceive you. For many shall come in my name, saying, I am Christ; and shall deceive many.**
142	*see that ye be not troubled:*	Matthew 24:6-8 And ye shall hear of wars and rumours of wars: **see that ye be not troubled:** for all these things must come to pass, but the end is not yet. For nation shall rise against nation, and kingdom against kingdom: and there shall be famines, and pestilences, and earthquakes, in divers places. All these are the beginning of sorrows.

Number	Commandment	Context of Commandment
143	*When ye therefore shall see the abomination of desolation, spoken of by Daniel the prophet, stand in the holy place, (whoso readeth, let him understand:) Then let them which be in Judaea flee into the mountains:*	Matthew 24:15-16 **When ye therefore shall see the abomination of desolation, spoken of by Daniel the prophet, stand in the holy place, (whoso readeth, let him understand:) Then let them which be in Judaea flee into the mountains:**
144	*Let him which is on the housetop not come down to take any thing out of his house:*	Matthew 24:17 **Let him which is on the housetop not come down to take any thing out of his house:**
145	*Neither let him which is in the field return back to take his clothes.*	Matthew 24:18 **Neither let him which is in the field return back to take his clothes.**
146	*pray ye that your flight be not in the winter, neither on the sabbath day:*	Matthew 24:19-21 And woe unto them that are with child, and to them that give suck in those days! But **pray ye that your flight be not in the winter, neither on the sabbath day:** For then shall be great tribulation, such as was not since the beginning of the world to this time, no, nor ever shall be.

Number	Commandment	Context of Commandment
147	*Then if any man shall say unto you, Lo, here is Christ, or there; believe it not.*	Matthew 24:22-24 And except those days should be shortened, there should no flesh be saved: but for the elect's sake those days shall be shortened. **Then if any man shall say unto you, Lo, here is Christ, or there; believe it not.** For there shall arise false Christs, and false prophets, and shall shew great signs and wonders; insomuch that, if it were possible, they shall deceive the very elect.
148	*Behold, I have told you before.*	Matthew 24:21-25 For then shall be great tribulation, such as was not since the beginning of the world to this time, no, nor ever shall be. And except those days should be shortened, there should no flesh be saved: but for the elect's sake those days shall be shortened. Then if any man shall say unto you, Lo, here is Christ, or there; believe it not. For there shall arise false Christs, and false prophets, and shall shew great signs and wonders; insomuch that, if it were possible, they shall deceive the very elect. **Behold, I have told you before.**
149	*believe it not.*	Matthew 24:26-28 Wherefore if they shall say unto you, Behold, he is in the desert; go not forth: behold, he is in the secret chambers; **believe it not.** For as the lightning cometh out of the east, and shineth even unto the west; so shall also the coming of the Son of man be. For wheresoever the carcase is, there will the eagles be gathered together.
150	*learn a parable of the fig tree;*	Matthew 24:32 Now **learn a parable of the fig tree;** When his branch is yet tender, and putteth forth leaves, ye know that summer is nigh:

Number	Commandment	Context of Commandment
151	*So likewise ye, when ye shall see all these things, know that it is near, even at the doors.*	Matthew 24:33-34 **So likewise ye, when ye shall see all these things, know that it is near, even at the doors.** Verily I say unto you, This generation shall not pass, till all these things be fulfilled.
152	*Watch therefore: for ye know not what hour your Lord doth come.*	Matthew 24:38-42 For as in the days that were before the flood they were eating and drinking, marrying and giving in marriage, until the day that Noe entered into the ark, And knew not until the flood came, and took them all away; so shall also the coming of the Son of man be. Then shall two be in the field; the one shall be taken, and the other left. Two women shall be grinding at the mill; the one shall be taken, and the other left. **Watch therefore: for ye know not what hour your Lord doth come.**
153	*know this, that if the goodman of the house had known in what watch the thief would come, he would have watched, and would not have suffered his house to be broken up.*	Matthew 24:43 But **know this, that if the goodman of the house had known in what watch the thief would come, he would have watched, and would not have suffered his house to be broken up.**
154	*Therefore be ye also ready:*	Matthew 24:44 **Therefore be ye also ready:** for in such an hour as ye think not the Son of man cometh.

Number	Commandment	Context of Commandment

Matthew 25:1-13

Then shall the kingdom of heaven be likened unto ten virgins, which took their lamps, and went forth to meet the bridegroom. And five of them were wise, and five were foolish. They that were foolish took their lamps, and took no oil with them: But the wise took oil in their vessels with their lamps. While the bridegroom tarried, they all slumbered and slept. And at midnight there was a cry made, Behold, the bridegroom cometh; go ye out to meet him. Then all those virgins arose, and trimmed their lamps. And the foolish said unto the wise, Give us of your oil; for our lamps are gone out. But the wise answered, saying, Not so; lest there be not enough for us and you: but go ye rather to them that sell, and buy for yourselves. And while they went to buy, the bridegroom came; and they that were ready went in with him to the marriage: and the door was shut. Afterward came also the other virgins, saying, Lord, Lord, open to us. But he answered and said, Verily I say unto you, I know you not. **Watch therefore, for ye know neither the day nor the hour wherein the Son of man cometh.**

155 — *Watch therefore, for ye know neither the day nor the hour wherein the Son of man cometh.*

---

156 — *Go into the city to such a man, and say unto him, The Master saith, My time is at hand; I will keep the passover at thy house with my disciples.*

Matthew 26:17-19

Now the first day of the feast of unleavened bread the disciples came to Jesus, saying unto him, Where wilt thou that we prepare for thee to eat the passover? And he said, **Go into the city to such a man, and say unto him, The Master saith, My time is at hand; I will keep the passover at thy house with my disciples.** And the disciples did as Jesus had appointed them; and they made ready the passover.

Number	Commandment	Context of Commandment
157	*Take, eat; this is my body.*	Matthew 26:26 And as they were eating, Jesus took bread, and blessed it, and brake it, and gave it to the disciples, and said, **Take, eat; this is my body.**
158	*Drink ye all of it;*	Matthew 26:27-28 And he took the cup, and gave thanks, and gave it to them, saying, **Drink ye all of it;** For this is my blood of the new testament, which is shed for many for the remission of sins.
159	*Sit ye here, while I go and pray yonder.*	Matthew 26:36 Then cometh Jesus with them unto a place called Gethsemane, and saith unto the disciples, **Sit ye here, while I go and pray yonder.**
160	*tarry ye here, and watch with me.*	Matthew 26:37-38 And he took with him Peter and the two sons of Zebedee, and began to be sorrowful and very heavy. Then saith he unto them, My soul is exceeding sorrowful, even unto death: **tarry ye here, and watch with me.**
161	*O my Father, if it be possible, let this cup pass from me:*	Matthew 26:39 And he went a little farther, and fell on his face, and prayed, saying, **O my Father, if it be possible, let this cup pass from me:** nevertheless not as I will, but as thou wilt.
162	*Watch and pray, that ye enter not into temptation:*	Matthew 26:40-41 And he cometh unto the disciples, and findeth them asleep, and saith unto Peter, What, could ye not watch with me one hour? **Watch and pray, that ye enter not into temptation:** the spirit indeed is willing, but the flesh is weak.

Number	Commandment	Context of Commandment
163	*O my Father, if this cup may not pass away from me, except I drink it, thy will be done.*	Matthew 26:42 He went away again the second time, and prayed, saying, **O my Father, if this cup may not pass away from me, except I drink it, thy will be done.**
164	*Sleep on now, and take your rest:*	Matthew 26:43-45 And he came and found them asleep again: for their eyes were heavy. And he left them, and went away again, and prayed the third time, saying the same words. Then cometh he to his disciples, and saith unto them, **Sleep on now, and take your rest:** behold, the hour is at hand, and the Son of man is betrayed into the hands of sinners.
165	*behold, the hour is at hand, and the Son of man is betrayed into the hands of sinners.*	Matthew 26:45 Then cometh he to his disciples, and saith unto them, Sleep on now, and take your rest: **behold, the hour is at hand, and the Son of man is betrayed into the hands of sinners.**
166	*Rise, let us be going:*	Matthew 26:46 **Rise, let us be going:** behold, he is at hand that doth betray me.
167	*behold, he is at hand that doth betray me.*	Matthew 26:46-47 Rise, let us be going: **behold, he is at hand that doth betray me.** And while he yet spake, lo, Judas, one of the twelve, came, and with him a great multitude with swords and staves, from the chief priests and elders of the people.

Number	Commandment	Context of Commandment
168	*Put up again thy sword into his place:*	Matthew 26:51-53 And, behold, one of them which were with Jesus stretched out his hand, and drew his sword, and struck a servant of the high priest's, and smote off his ear. Then said Jesus unto him, **Put up again thy sword into his place:** for all they that take the sword shall perish with the sword. Thinkest thou that I cannot now pray to my Father, and he shall presently give me more than twelve legions of angels?
169	*All hail.*	Matthew 28:9 And as they went to tell his disciples, behold, Jesus met them, saying, **All hail.** And they came and held him by the feet, and worshipped him.
170	*Be not afraid:*	Matthew 28:10 Then said Jesus unto them, **Be not afraid:** go tell my brethren that they go into Galilee, and there shall they see me.
171	*go tell my brethren that they go into Galilee, and there shall they see me.*	Matthew 28:10 Then said Jesus unto them, Be not afraid: **go tell my brethren that they go into Galilee, and there shall they see me.**
172	*Go ye therefore, and teach all nations, baptizing them in the name of the Father, and of the Son, and of the Holy Ghost: Teaching them to observe all things whatsoever I have commanded you:*	Matthew 28:18-20 And Jesus came and spake unto them, saying, All power is given unto me in heaven and in earth. **Go ye therefore, and teach all nations, baptizing them in the name of the Father, and of the Son, and of the Holy Ghost: Teaching them to observe all things whatsoever I have commanded you:** and, lo, I am with you always, even unto the end of the world. Amen.

Commandments
of Jesus Christ
found in:

THE GOSPEL
ACCORDING
TO MARK

Number	Commandment	Context of Commandment
173	*repent ye, and believe the gospel.*	Mark 1:14-15 Now after that John was put in prison, Jesus came into Galilee, preaching the gospel of the kingdom of God, And saying, The time is fulfilled, and the kingdom of God is at hand: **repent ye, and believe the gospel.**
174	*Come ye after me, and I will make you to become fishers of men.*	Mark 1:16-18 Now as he walked by the sea of Galilee, he saw Simon and Andrew his brother casting a net into the sea: for they were fishers. And Jesus said unto them, **Come ye after me, and I will make you to become fishers of men.** And straightway they forsook their nets, and followed him.
175	*Let us go into the next towns, that I may preach there also: for therefore came I forth.*	Mark 1:36-38 And Simon and they that were with him followed after him. And when they had found him, they said unto him, All men seek for thee. And he said unto them, **Let us go into the next towns, that I may preach there also: for therefore came I forth.**
176	*See thou say nothing to any man:*	Mark 1:40-44 And there came a leper to him, beseeching him, and kneeling down to him, and saying unto him, If thou wilt, thou canst make me clean. And Jesus, moved with compassion, put forth his hand, and touched him, and saith unto him, I will; be thou clean. And as soon as he had spoken, immediately the leprosy departed from him, and he was cleansed. And he straitly charged him, and forthwith sent him away; And saith unto him, **See thou say nothing to any man:** but go thy way, shew thyself to the priest, and offer for thy cleansing those things which Moses commanded, for a testimony unto them.

Number	Commandment	Context of Commandment
177	*offer for thy cleansing those things which Moses commanded, for a testimony unto them.*	Mark 1:44-45 And saith unto him, See thou say nothing to any man: but go thy way, shew thyself to the priest, and **offer for thy cleansing those things which Moses commanded, for a testimony unto them.** But he went out, and began to publish it much, and to blaze abroad the matter, insomuch that Jesus could no more openly enter into the city, but was without in desert places: and they came to him from every quarter.
178	*take up thy bed, and go thy way into thine house.*	Mark 2:3-11 And they come unto him, bringing one sick of the palsy, which was borne of four. And when they could not come nigh unto him for the press, they uncovered the roof where he was: and when they had broken it up, they let down the bed wherein the sick of the palsy lay. When Jesus saw their faith, he said unto the sick of the palsy, Son, thy sins be forgiven thee. But there was certain of the scribes sitting there, and reasoning in their hearts, Why doth this man thus speak blasphemies? who can forgive sins but God only? And immediately when Jesus perceived in his spirit that they so reasoned within themselves, he said unto them, Why reason ye these things in your hearts? Whether is it easier to say to the sick of the palsy, Thy sins be forgiven thee; or to say, Arise, and take up thy bed, and walk? But that ye may know that the Son of man hath power on earth to forgive sins, (he saith to the sick of the palsy,) I say unto thee, Arise, and **take up thy bed, and go thy way into thine house.**
179	*Follow me.*	Mark 2:13-14 And he went forth again by the sea side; and all the multitude resorted unto him, and he taught them. And as he passed by, he saw Levi the son of Alphaeus sitting at the receipt of custom, and said unto him, **Follow me.** And he arose and followed him.

Number	Commandment	Context of Commandment
180	*Hearken; Behold, there went out a sower to sow: And it came to pass, as he sowed, some fell by the way side, and the fowls of the air came and devoured it up. And some fell on stony ground, where it had not much earth; and immediately it sprang up, because it had no depth of earth: But when the sun was up, it was scorched; and because it had no root, it withered away. And some fell among thorns, and the thorns grew up, and choked it, and it yielded no fruit. And other fell on good ground, and did yield fruit that sprang up and increased; and brought forth, some thirty, and some sixty, and some an hundred.*	Mark 4:2-8 And he taught them many things by parables, and said unto them in his doctrine, **Hearken; Behold, there went out a sower to sow: And it came to pass, as he sowed, some fell by the way side, and the fowls of the air came and devoured it up. And some fell on stony ground, where it had not much earth; and immediately it sprang up, because it had no depth of earth: But when the sun was up, it was scorched; and because it had no root, it withered away. And some fell among thorns, and the thorns grew up, and choked it, and it yielded no fruit. And other fell on good ground, and did yield fruit that sprang up and increased; and brought forth, some thirty, and some sixty, and some an hundred.**

Number	Commandment	Context of Commandment
181	*He that hath ears to hear, let him hear.*	Mark 4:3-9 Hearken; Behold, there went out a sower to sow: And it came to pass, as he sowed, some fell by the way side, and the fowls of the air came and devoured it up. And some fell on stony ground, where it had not much earth; and immediately it sprang up, because it had no depth of earth: But when the sun was up, it was scorched; and because it had no root, it withered away. And some fell among thorns, and the thorns grew up, and choked it, and it yielded no fruit. And other fell on good ground, and did yield fruit that sprang up and increased; and brought forth, some thirty, and some sixty, and some an hundred. And he said unto them, **He that hath ears to hear, let him hear.**
182	*If any man have ears to hear, let him hear.*	Mark 4:14-23 The sower soweth the word. And these are they by the way side, where the word is sown; but when they have heard, Satan cometh immediately, and taketh away the word that was sown in their hearts. And these are they likewise which are sown on stony ground; who, when they have heard the word, immediately receive it with gladness; And have no root in themselves, and so endure but for a time: afterward, when affliction or persecution ariseth for the word's sake, immediately they are offended. And these are they which are sown among thorns; such as hear the word, And the cares of this world, and the deceitfulness of riches, and the lusts of other things entering in, choke the word, and it becometh unfruitful. And these are they which are sown on good ground; such as hear the word, and receive it, and bring forth fruit, some thirtyfold, some sixty, and some an hundred. And he said unto them, Is a candle brought to be put under a bushel, or under a bed? and not to be set on a candlestick? For there is nothing hid, which shall not be manifested; neither was any thing kept secret, but that it should come abroad. **If any man have ears to hear, let him hear.**

Number	Commandment	Context of Commandment
183	*Take heed what ye hear:*	Mark 4:24-25 And he said unto them, **Take heed what ye hear:** with what measure ye mete, it shall be measured to you: and unto you that hear shall more be given. For he that hath, to him shall be given: and he that hath not, from him shall be taken even that which he hath.
184	*Let us pass over unto the other side.*	Mark 4:35-36 And the same day, when the even was come, he saith unto them, **Let us pass over unto the other side.** And when they had sent away the multitude, they took him even as he was in the ship. And there were also with him other little ships.
185	*Peace, be still.*	Mark 4:37-41 And there arose a great storm of wind, and the waves beat into the ship, so that it was now full. And he was in the hinder part of the ship, asleep on a pillow: and they awake him, and say unto him, Master, carest thou not that we perish? And he arose, and rebuked the wind, and said unto the sea, **Peace, be still.** And the wind ceased, and there was a great calm. And he said unto them, Why are ye so fearful? how is it that ye have no faith? And they feared exceedingly, and said one to another, What manner of man is this, that even the wind and the sea obey him?

Number	Commandment	Context of Commandment
186	*Come out of the man, thou unclean spirit.*	Mark 5:2-8 And when he was come out of the ship, immediately there met him out of the tombs a man with an unclean spirit, Who had his dwelling among the tombs; and no man could bind him, no, not with chains: Because that he had been often bound with fetters and chains, and the chains had been plucked asunder by him, and the fetters broken in pieces: neither could any man tame him. And always, night and day, he was in the mountains, and in the tombs, crying, and cutting himself with stones. But when he saw Jesus afar off, he ran and worshipped him, And cried with a loud voice, and said, What have I to do with thee, Jesus, thou Son of the most high God? I adjure thee by God, that thou torment me not. For he said unto him, **Come out of the man, thou unclean spirit.**

Number	Commandment	Context of Commandment

Mark 5:9-20

And he asked him, What is thy name? And he answered, saying, My name is Legion: for we are many. And he besought him much that he would not send them away out of the country. Now there was there nigh unto the mountains a great herd of swine feeding. And all the devils besought him, saying, Send us into the swine, that we may enter into them. And forthwith Jesus gave them leave. And the unclean spirits went out, and entered into the swine: and the herd ran violently down a steep place into the sea, (they were about two thousand;) and were choked in the sea. And they that fed the swine fled, and told it in the city, and in the country. And they went out to see what it was that was done. And they come to Jesus, and see him that was possessed with the devil, and had the legion, sitting, and clothed, and in his right mind: and they were afraid. And they that saw it told them how it befell to him that was possessed with the devil, and also concerning the swine. And they began to pray him to depart out of their coasts. And when he was come into the ship, he that had been possessed with the devil prayed him that he might be with him. Howbeit Jesus suffered him not, but saith unto him, **Go home to thy friends, and tell them how great things the Lord hath done for thee, and hath had compassion on thee.** And he departed, and began to publish in Decapolis how great things Jesus had done for him: and all men did marvel.

187 *Go home to thy friends, and tell them how great things the Lord hath done for thee, and hath had compassion on thee.*

Number	Commandment	Context of Commandment
188	*go in peace,*	Mark 5:25-34 And a certain woman, which had an issue of blood twelve years, And had suffered many things of many physicians, and had spent all that she had, and was nothing bettered, but rather grew worse, When she had heard of Jesus, came in the press behind, and touched his garment. For she said, If I may touch but his clothes, I shall be whole. And straightway the fountain of her blood was dried up; and she felt in her body that she was healed of that plague. And Jesus, immediately knowing in himself that virtue had gone out of him, turned him about in the press, and said, Who touched my clothes? And his disciples said unto him, Thou seest the multitude thronging thee, and sayest thou, Who touched me? And he looked round about to see her that had done this thing. But the woman fearing and trembling, knowing what was done in her, came and fell down before him, and told him all the truth. And he said unto her, Daughter, thy faith hath made thee whole; **go in peace,** and be whole of thy plague.
189	*be whole of thy plague.*	Mark 5:34 And he said unto her, Daughter, thy faith hath made thee whole; go in peace, and **be whole of thy plague.**
190	*Be not afraid, only believe.*	Mark 5:35-36 While he yet spake, there came from the ruler of the synagogue's house certain which said, Thy daughter is dead: why troublest thou the Master any further? As soon as Jesus heard the word that was spoken, he saith unto the ruler of the synagogue, **Be not afraid, only believe.**

Number	Commandment	Context of Commandment
191	*Talitha cumi; which is, being interpreted, Damsel, I say unto thee, arise.*	Mark 5:37-42 And he suffered no man to follow him, save Peter, and James, and John the brother of James. And he cometh to the house of the ruler of the synagogue, and seeth the tumult, and them that wept and wailed greatly. And when he was come in, he saith unto them, Why make ye this ado, and weep? the damsel is not dead, but sleepeth. And they laughed him to scorn. But when he had put them all out, he taketh the father and the mother of the damsel, and them that were with him, and entereth in where the damsel was lying. And he took the damsel by the hand, and said unto her, **Talitha cumi; which is, being interpreted, Damsel, I say unto thee, arise.** And straightway the damsel arose, and walked; for she was of the age of twelve years. And they were astonished with a great astonishment.
192	*In what place soever ye enter into an house, there abide till ye depart from that place.*	Mark 6:7-10 And he called unto him the twelve, and began to send them forth by two and two; and gave them power over unclean spirits; And commanded them that they should take nothing for their journey, save a staff only; no scrip, no bread, no money in their purse: But be shod with sandals; and not put on two coats. And he said unto them, **In what place soever ye enter into an house, there abide till ye depart from that place.**
193	*whosoever shall not receive you, nor hear you, when ye depart thence, shake off the dust under your feet for a testimony against them.*	Mark 6:11 And **whosoever shall not receive you, nor hear you, when ye depart thence, shake off the dust under your feet for a testimony against them.** Verily I say unto you, It shall be more tolerable for Sodom and Gomorrha in the day of judgment, than for that city.

Number	Commandment	Context of Commandment
194	*Come ye yourselves apart into a desert place, and rest a while:*	Mark 6:30-32 And the apostles gathered themselves together unto Jesus, and told him all things, both what they had done, and what they had taught. And he said unto them, **Come ye yourselves apart into a desert place, and rest a while:** for there were many coming and going, and they had no leisure so much as to eat. And they departed into a desert place by ship privately.
195	*go and see.*	Mark 6:33-39 And the people saw them departing, and many knew him, and ran afoot thither out of all cities, and outwent them, and came together unto him. And Jesus, when he came out, saw much people, and was moved with compassion toward them, because they were as sheep not having a shepherd: and he began to teach them many things. And when the day was now far spent, his disciples came unto him, and said, This is a desert place, and now the time is far passed: Send them away, that they may go into the country round about, and into the villages, and buy themselves bread: for they have nothing to eat. He answered and said unto them, Give ye them to eat. And they say unto him, Shall we go and buy two hundred pennyworth of bread, and give them to eat? He saith unto them, How many loaves have ye? **go and see.** And when they knew, they say, Five, and two fishes. And he commanded them to make all sit down by companies upon the green grass.
196	*Hearken unto me every one of you, and understand: There is nothing from without a man, that entering into him can defile him: but the things which come out of him, those are they that defile the man.*	Mark 7:14-15 And when he had called all the people unto him, he said unto them, **Hearken unto me every one of you, and understand: There is nothing from without a man, that entering into him can defile him: but the things which come out of him, those are they that defile the man.**

Commandments of Jesus Christ found in: The Gospel According To Mark

Number	Commandment	Context of Commandment
197	*If any man have ears to hear, let him hear.*	Mark 7:14-16 And when he had called all the people unto him, he said unto them, Hearken unto me every one of you, and understand: There is nothing from without a man, that entering into him can defile him: but the things which come out of him, those are they that defile the man. **If any man have ears to hear, let him hear.**
198	*Let the children first be filled: for it is not meet to take the children's bread, and to cast it unto the dogs.*	Mark 7:25-27 For a certain woman, whose young daughter had an unclean spirit, heard of him, and came and fell at his feet: The woman was a Greek, a Syrophenician by nation; and she besought him that he would cast forth the devil out of her daughter. But Jesus said unto her, **Let the children first be filled: for it is not meet to take the children's bread, and to cast it unto the dogs.**
199	*For this saying go thy way; the devil is gone out of thy daughter.*	Mark 7:28-30 And she answered and said unto him, Yes, Lord: yet the dogs under the table eat of the children's crumbs. And he said unto her, **For this saying go thy way; the devil is gone out of thy daughter.** And when she was come to her house, she found the devil gone out, and her daughter laid upon the bed.
200	*Ephphatha, that is, Be opened.*	Mark 7:32-35 And they bring unto him one that was deaf, and had an impediment in his speech; and they beseech him to put his hand upon him. And he took him aside from the multitude, and put his fingers into his ears, and he spit, and touched his tongue; And looking up to heaven, he sighed, and saith unto him, **Ephphatha, that is, Be opened.** And straightway his ears were opened, and the string of his tongue was loosed, and he spake plain.
201	*Take heed, beware of the leaven of the Pharisees, and of the leaven of Herod.*	Mark 8:14-15 Now the disciples had forgotten to take bread, neither had they in the ship with them more than one loaf. And he charged them, saying, **Take heed, beware of the leaven of the Pharisees, and of the leaven of Herod.**

Number	Commandment	Context of Commandment
202	*Neither go into the town, nor tell it to any in the town.*	Mark 8:23-26 And he took the blind man by the hand, and led him out of the town; and when he had spit on his eyes, and put his hands upon him, he asked him if he saw ought. And he looked up, and said, I see men as trees, walking. After that he put his hands again upon his eyes, and made him look up: and he was restored, and saw every man clearly. And he sent him away to his house, saying, **Neither go into the town, nor tell it to any in the town.**
203	*bring him unto me.*	Mark 9:17-19 And one of the multitude answered and said, Master, I have brought unto thee my son, which hath a dumb spirit; And wheresoever he taketh him, he teareth him: and he foameth, and gnasheth with his teeth, and pineth away: and I spake to thy disciples that they should cast him out; and they could not. He answereth him, and saith, O faithless generation, how long shall I be with you? how long shall I suffer you? **bring him unto me.**
204	*Thou dumb and deaf spirit, I charge thee, come out of him,*	Mark 9:25 When Jesus saw that the people came running together, he rebuked the foul spirit, saying unto him, **Thou dumb and deaf spirit, I charge thee, come out of him,** and enter no more into him.
205	*enter no more into him.*	Mark 9:25-27 When Jesus saw that the people came running together, he rebuked the foul spirit, saying unto him, Thou dumb and deaf spirit, I charge thee, come out of him, and **enter no more into him.** And the spirit cried, and rent him sore, and came out of him: and he was as one dead; insomuch that many said, He is dead. But Jesus took him by the hand, and lifted him up; and he arose.

Commandments of Jesus Christ found in: The Gospel According To Mark

Number	Commandment	Context of Commandment
206	*Forbid him not:*	Mark 9:38-40 And John answered him, saying, Master, we saw one casting out devils in thy name, and he followeth not us: and we forbad him, because he followeth not us. But Jesus said, **Forbid him not:** for there is no man which shall do a miracle in my name, that can lightly speak evil of me. For he that is not against us is on our part.
207	*if thy hand offend thee, cut it off:*	Mark 9:42-44 And whosoever shall offend one of these little ones that believe in me, it is better for him that a millstone were hanged about his neck, and he were cast into the sea. And **if thy hand offend thee, cut it off:** it is better for thee to enter into life maimed, than having two hands to go into hell, into the fire that never shall be quenched: Where their worm dieth not, and the fire is not quenched.
208	*if thy foot offend thee, cut it off:*	Mark 9:45-46 And **if thy foot offend thee, cut it off:** it is better for thee to enter halt into life, than having two feet to be cast into hell, into the fire that never shall be quenched: Where their worm dieth not, and the fire is not quenched.
209	*if thine eye offend thee, pluck it out:*	Mark 9:47-48 And **if thine eye offend thee, pluck it out:** it is better for thee to enter into the kingdom of God with one eye, than having two eyes to be cast into hell fire: Where their worm dieth not, and the fire is not quenched.
210	*Have salt in yourselves,*	Mark 9:49-50 For every one shall be salted with fire, and every sacrifice shall be salted with salt. Salt is good: but if the salt have lost his saltness, wherewith will ye season it? **Have salt in yourselves,** and have peace one with another.

Number	Commandment	Context of Commandment
211	*have peace one with another.*	Mark 9:50 Salt is good: but if the salt have lost his saltness, wherewith will ye season it? Have salt in yourselves, and **have peace one with another.**
212	*go thy way, sell whatsoever thou hast, and give to the poor, and thou shalt have treasure in heaven: and come, take up the cross, and follow me.*	Mark 10:17-22 And when he was gone forth into the way, there came one running, and kneeled to him, and asked him, Good Master, what shall I do that I may inherit eternal life? And Jesus said unto him, Why callest thou me good? there is none good but one, that is, God. Thou knowest the commandments, Do not commit adultery, Do not kill, Do not steal, Do not bear false witness, Defraud not, Honour thy father and mother. And he answered and said unto him, Master, all these have I observed from my youth. Then Jesus beholding him loved him, and said unto him, One thing thou lackest: **go thy way, sell whatsoever thou hast, and give to the poor, and thou shalt have treasure in heaven: and come, take up the cross, and follow me.** And he was sad at that saying, and went away grieved: for he had great possessions.
213	*Go thy way;*	Mark 10:46-52 And they came to Jericho: and as he went out of Jericho with his disciples and a great number of people, blind Bartimaeus, the son of Timaeus, sat by the highway side begging. And when he heard that it was Jesus of Nazareth, he began to cry out, and say, Jesus, thou son of David, have mercy on me. And many charged him that he should hold his peace: but he cried the more a great deal, Thou son of David, have mercy on me. And Jesus stood still, and commanded him to be called. And they call the blind man, saying unto him, Be of good comfort, rise; he calleth thee. And he, casting away his garment, rose, and came to Jesus. And Jesus answered and said unto him, What wilt thou that I should do unto thee? The blind man said unto him, Lord, that I might receive my sight. And Jesus said unto him, **Go thy way;** thy faith hath made thee whole. And immediately he received his sight, and followed Jesus in the way.

Number	Commandment	Context of Commandment
214	*Go your way into the village over against you: and as soon as ye be entered into it, ye shall find a colt tied, whereon never man sat;*	Mark 11:1-2 And when they came nigh to Jerusalem, unto Bethphage and Bethany, at the mount of Olives, he sendeth forth two of his disciples, And saith unto them, **Go your way into the village over against you: and as soon as ye be entered into it, ye shall find a colt tied, whereon never man sat;** loose him, and bring him.
215	*loose him,*	Mark 11:2 And saith unto them, Go your way into the village over against you: and as soon as ye be entered into it, ye shall find a colt tied, whereon never man sat; **loose him,** and bring him.
216	*bring him.*	Mark 11:2 And saith unto them, Go your way into the village over against you: and as soon as ye be entered into it, ye shall find a colt tied, whereon never man sat; loose him, and **bring him.**
217	*And if any man say unto you, Why do ye this? say ye that the Lord hath need of him;*	Mark 11:3 **And if any man say unto you, Why do ye this? say ye that the Lord hath need of him;** and straightway he will send him hither.
218	*Have faith in God.*	Mark 11:20-23 And in the morning, as they passed by, they saw the fig tree dried up from the roots. And Peter calling to remembrance saith unto him, Master, behold, the fig tree which thou cursedst is withered away. And Jesus answering saith unto them, **Have faith in God.** For verily I say unto you, That whosoever shall say unto this mountain, Be thou removed, and be thou cast into the sea; and shall not doubt in his heart, but shall believe that those things which he saith shall come to pass; he shall have whatsoever he saith.

Number	Commandment	Context of Commandment
219	*What things soever ye desire, when ye pray, believe that ye receive them, and ye shall have them.*	Mark 11:24 Therefore I say unto you, **What things soever ye desire, when ye pray, believe that ye receive them, and ye shall have them.**
220	*when ye stand praying, forgive, if ye have ought against any: that your Father also which is in heaven may forgive you your trespasses.*	Mark 11:25-26 And **when ye stand praying, forgive, if ye have ought against any: that your Father also which is in heaven may forgive you your trespasses.** But if ye do not forgive, neither will your Father which is in heaven forgive your trespasses.
221	*answer me.*	Mark 11:28-30 And say unto him, By what authority doest thou these things? and who gave thee this authority to do these things? And Jesus answered and said unto them, I will also ask of you one question, and answer me, and I will tell you by what authority I do these things. The baptism of John, was it from heaven, or of men? **answer me.**
222	*bring me a penny, that I may see it.*	Mark 12:14-15 And when they were come, they say unto him, Master, we know that thou art true, and carest for no man: for thou regardest not the person of men, but teachest the way of God in truth: Is it lawful to give tribute to Caesar, or not? Shall we give, or shall we not give? But he, knowing their hypocrisy, said unto them, Why tempt ye me? **bring me a penny, that I may see it.**

Number	Commandment	Context of Commandment
223	*Beware of the scribes, which love to go in long clothing, and love salutations in the marketplaces, And the chief seats in the synagogues, and the uppermost rooms at feasts: Which devour widows' houses, and for a pretence make long prayers:*	Mark 12:38-40 And he said unto them in his doctrine, **Beware of the scribes, which love to go in long clothing, and love salutations in the marketplaces, And the chief seats in the synagogues, and the uppermost rooms at feasts: Which devour widows' houses, and for a pretence make long prayers:** these shall receive greater damnation.
224	*take heed to yourselves: for they shall deliver you up to councils; and in the synagogues ye shall be beaten: and ye shall be brought before rulers and kings for my sake, for a testimony against them.*	Mark 13:8-9 For nation shall rise against nation, and kingdom against kingdom: and there shall be earthquakes in divers places, and there shall be famines and troubles: these are the beginnings of sorrows. But **take heed to yourselves: for they shall deliver you up to councils; and in the synagogues ye shall be beaten: and ye shall be brought before rulers and kings for my sake, for a testimony against them.**

Number	Commandment	Context of Commandment
225	*when they shall lead you, and deliver you up, take no thought beforehand what ye shall speak, neither do ye premeditate:*	Mark 13:11 But **when they shall lead you, and deliver you up, take no thought beforehand what ye shall speak, neither do ye premeditate:** but whatsoever shall be given you in that hour, that speak ye: for it is not ye that speak, but the Holy Ghost.
226	*whatsoever shall be given you in that hour, that speak ye:*	Mark 13:11 But when they shall lead you, and deliver you up, take no thought beforehand what ye shall speak, neither do ye premeditate: but **whatsoever shall be given you in that hour, that speak ye:** for it is not ye that speak, but the Holy Ghost.
227	*let him that is on the housetop not go down into the house, neither enter therein, to take any thing out of his house:*	Mark 13:14-16 But when ye shall see the abomination of desolation, spoken of by Daniel the prophet, standing where it ought not, (let him that readeth understand,) then let them that be in Judaea flee to the mountains: And **let him that is on the housetop not go down into the house, neither enter therein, to take any thing out of his house:** And let him that is in the field not turn back again for to take up his garment.
228	*if any man shall say to you, Lo, here is Christ; or, lo, he is there; believe him not:*	Mark 13:21-22 And then **if any man shall say to you, Lo, here is Christ; or, lo, he is there; believe him not:** For false Christs and false prophets shall rise, and shall shew signs and wonders, to seduce, if it were possible, even the elect.
229	*take ye heed: behold, I have foretold you all things.*	Mark 13:23 But **take ye heed: behold, I have foretold you all things.**

Number	Commandment	Context of Commandment
230	*Take ye heed, watch and pray: for ye know not when the time is.*	Mark 13:30-33 Verily I say unto you, that this generation shall not pass, till all these things be done. Heaven and earth shall pass away: but my words shall not pass away. But of that day and that hour knoweth no man, no, not the angels which are in heaven, neither the Son, but the Father. **Take ye heed, watch and pray: for ye know not when the time is.**
231	*Watch ye therefore: for ye know not when the master of the house cometh, at even, or at midnight, or at the cockcrowing, or in the morning:*	Mark 13:34-36 For the Son of Man is as a man taking a far journey, who left his house, and gave authority to his servants, and to every man his work, and commanded the porter to watch. **Watch ye therefore: for ye know not when the master of the house cometh, at even, or at midnight, or at the cockcrowing, or in the morning:** Lest coming suddenly he find you sleeping.
232	*Watch.*	Mark 13:37 And what I say unto you I say unto all, **Watch.**
233	*Let her alone;*	Mark 14:3-9 And being in Bethany in the house of Simon the leper, as he sat at meat, there came a woman having an alabaster box of ointment of spikenard very precious; and she brake the box, and poured it on his head. And there were some that had indignation within themselves, and said, Why was this waste of the ointment made? For it might have been sold for more than three hundred pence, and have been given to the poor. And they murmured against her. And Jesus said, **Let her alone;** why trouble ye her? she hath wrought a good work on me. For ye have the poor with you always, and whensoever ye will ye may do them good: but me ye have not always. She hath done what she could: she is come aforehand to anoint my body to the burying. Verily I say unto you, Wheresoever this gospel shall be preached throughout the whole world, this also that she hath done shall be spoken of for a memorial of her.

Number	Commandment	Context of Commandment
234	*Go ye into the city, and there shall meet you a man bearing a pitcher of water: follow him.*	Mark 14:12-13 And the first day of unleavened bread, when they killed the passover, his disciples said unto him, Where wilt thou that we go and prepare that thou mayest eat the passover? And he sendeth forth two of his disciples, and saith unto them, **Go ye into the city, and there shall meet you a man bearing a pitcher of water: follow him.**
235	*say ye to the goodman of the house, The Master saith, Where is the guestchamber, where I shall eat the passover with my disciples?*	Mark 14:14 And wheresoever he shall go in, **say ye to the goodman of the house, The Master saith, Where is the guestchamber, where I shall eat the passover with my disciples?**
236	*there make ready for us.*	Mark 14:15-16 And he will shew you a large upper room furnished and prepared: **there make ready for us.** And his disciples went forth, and came into the city, and found as he had said unto them: and they made ready the passover.
237	*Abba, Father, all things are possible unto thee; take away this cup from me: nevertheless not what I will, but what thou wilt.*	Mark 14:33-36 And he taketh with him Peter and James and John, and began to be sore amazed, and to be very heavy; And saith unto them, My soul is exceeding sorrowful unto death: tarry ye here, and watch. And he went forward a little, and fell on the ground, and prayed that, if it were possible, the hour might pass from him. And he said, **Abba, Father, all things are possible unto thee; take away this cup from me: nevertheless not what I will, but what thou wilt.**

Number	Commandment	Context of Commandment
238	*Go ye into all the world, and preach the gospel to every creature.*	Mark 16:14-16 Afterward he appeared unto the eleven as they sat at meat, and upbraided them with their unbelief and hardness of heart, because they believed not them which had seen him after he was risen. And he said unto them, **Go ye into all the world, and preach the gospel to every creature.** He that believeth and is baptized shall be saved; but he that believeth not shall be damned.

Commandments
of Jesus Christ
found in:

THE GOSPEL
ACCORDING
TO LUKE

Number	Commandment	Context of Commandment
239	*Get thee behind me, Satan:*	Luke 4:5-8 And the devil, taking him up into an high mountain, shewed unto him all the kingdoms of the world in a moment of time. And the devil said unto him, All this power will I give thee, and the glory of them: for that is delivered unto me; and to whomsoever I will I give it. If thou therefore wilt worship me, all shall be thine. And Jesus answered and said unto him, **Get thee behind me, Satan:** for it is written, Thou shalt worship the Lord thy God, and him only shalt thou serve.
240	*Hold thy peace, and come out of him.*	Luke 4:33-37 And in the synagogue there was a man, which had a spirit of an unclean devil, and cried out with a loud voice, Saying, Let us alone; what have we to do with thee, thou Jesus of Nazareth? art thou come to destroy us? I know thee who thou art; the Holy One of God. And Jesus rebuked him, saying, **Hold thy peace, and come out of him.** And when the devil had thrown him in the midst, he came out of him, and hurt him not. And they were all amazed, and spake among themselves, saying, What a word is this! for with authority and power he commandeth the unclean spirits, and they come out. And the fame of him went out into every place of the country round about.
241	*Launch out into the deep, and let down your nets for a draught.*	Luke 5:3-4 And he entered into one of the ships, which was Simon's, and prayed him that he would thrust out a little from the land. And he sat down, and taught the people out of the ship. Now when he had left speaking, he said unto Simon, **Launch out into the deep, and let down your nets for a draught.**

Number	Commandment	Context of Commandment

Luke 5:5-11

And Simon answering said unto him, Master, we have toiled all the night, and have taken nothing: nevertheless at thy word I will let down the net. And when they had this done, they inclosed a great multitude of fishes: and their net brake. And they beckoned unto their partners, which were in the other ship, that they should come and help them. And they came, and filled both the ships, so that they began to sink. When Simon Peter saw it, he fell down at Jesus' knees, saying, Depart from me; for I am a sinful man, O Lord. For he was astonished, and all that were with him, at the draught of the fishes which they had taken: And so was also James, and John, the sons of Zebedee, which were partners with Simon. And Jesus said unto Simon, **Fear not; from henceforth thou shalt catch men.** And when they had brought their ships to land, they forsook all, and followed him.

242 — *Fear not; from henceforth thou shalt catch men.*

Luke 5:18-25

And, behold, men brought in a bed a man which was taken with a palsy: and they sought means to bring him in, and to lay him before him. And when they could not find by what way they might bring him in because of the multitude, they went upon the housetop, and let him down through the tiling with his couch into the midst before Jesus. And when he saw their faith, he said unto him, Man, thy sins are forgiven thee. And the scribes and the Pharisees began to reason, saying, Who is this which speaketh blasphemies? Who can forgive sins, but God alone? But when Jesus perceived their thoughts, he answering said unto them, What reason ye in your hearts? Whether is easier, to say, Thy sins be forgiven thee; or to say, Rise up and walk? But that ye may know that the Son of man hath power upon earth to forgive sins, (he said unto the sick of the palsy,) I say unto thee, **Arise, and take up thy couch, and go into thine house.** And immediately he rose up before them, and took up that whereon he lay, and departed to his own house, glorifying God.

243 — *Arise, and take up thy couch, and go into thine house.*

Number	Commandment	Context of Commandment
244	*Rise up, and stand forth in the midst.*	Luke 6:6-8 And it came to pass also on another sabbath, that he entered into the synagogue and taught: and there was a man whose right hand was withered. And the scribes and Pharisees watched him, whether he would heal on the sabbath day; that they might find an accusation against him. But he knew their thoughts, and said to the man which had the withered hand, **Rise up, and stand forth in the midst.** And he arose and stood forth.
245	*Stretch forth thy hand.*	Luke 6:9-11 Then said Jesus unto them, I will ask you one thing; Is it lawful on the sabbath days to do good, or to do evil? to save life, or to destroy it? And looking round about upon them all, he said unto the man, **Stretch forth thy hand.** And he did so: and his hand was restored whole as the other. And they were filled with madness; and communed one with another what they might do to Jesus.
246	*Rejoice ye in that day, and leap for joy:*	Luke 6:22-23 Blessed are ye, when men shall hate you, and when they shall separate you from their company, and shall reproach you, and cast out your name as evil, for the Son of man's sake. **Rejoice ye in that day, and leap for joy:** for, behold, your reward is great in heaven: for in the like manner did their fathers unto the prophets.
247	*behold, your reward is great in heaven:*	Luke 6:23 Rejoice ye in that day, and leap for joy: for, **behold, your reward is great in heaven:** for in the like manner did their fathers unto the prophets.

Number	Commandment	Context of Commandment
248	*forbid not to take thy coat also.*	Luke 6:27-29 But I say unto you which hear, Love your enemies, do good to them which hate you, Bless them that curse you, and pray for them which despitefully use you. And unto him that smiteth thee on the one cheek offer also the other; and him that taketh away thy cloak **forbid not to take thy coat also.**
249	*Give to every man that asketh of thee;*	Luke 6:30 **Give to every man that asketh of thee;** and of him that taketh away thy goods ask them not again.
250	*of him that taketh away thy goods ask them not again.*	Luke 6:30 Give to every man that asketh of thee; and **of him that taketh away thy goods ask them not again.**
251	*as ye would that men should do to you, do ye also to them likewise.*	Luke 6:31 And **as ye would that men should do to you, do ye also to them likewise.**
252	*do good,*	Luke 6:32-35 For if ye love them which love you, what thank have ye? for sinners also love those that love them. And if ye do good to them which do good to you, what thank have ye? for sinners also do even the same. And if ye lend to them of whom ye hope to receive, what thank have ye? for sinners also lend to sinners, to receive as much again. But love ye your enemies, and **do good,** and lend, hoping for nothing again; and your reward shall be great, and ye shall be the children of the Highest: for he is kind unto the unthankful and to the evil.

Number	Commandment	Context of Commandment
253	*lend, hoping for nothing again;*	Luke 6:35 But love ye your enemies, and do good, and **lend, hoping for nothing again;** and your reward shall be great, and ye shall be the children of the Highest: for he is kind unto the unthankful and to the evil.
254	*Be ye therefore merciful, as your Father also is merciful.*	Luke 6:36 **Be ye therefore merciful, as your Father also is merciful.**
255	*condemn not, and ye shall not be condemned:*	Luke 6:37 Judge not, and ye shall not be judged: **condemn not, and ye shall not be condemned:** forgive, and ye shall be forgiven:
256	*forgive, and ye shall be forgiven:*	Luke 6:37 Judge not, and ye shall not be judged: condemn not, and ye shall not be condemned: **forgive, and ye shall be forgiven:**
257	*Give, and it shall be given unto you; good measure, pressed down, and shaken together, and running over, shall men give into your bosom.*	Luke 6:38 **Give, and it shall be given unto you; good measure, pressed down, and shaken together, and running over, shall men give into your bosom.** For with the same measure that ye mete withal it shall be measured to you again.
258	*Weep not.*	Luke 7:12-13 Now when he came nigh to the gate of the city, behold, there was a dead man carried out, the only son of his mother, and she was a widow: and much people of the city was with her. And when the Lord saw her, he had compassion on her, and said unto her, **Weep not.**

Number	Commandment	Context of Commandment
259	*Young man, I say unto thee, Arise.*	Luke 7:14-16 And he came and touched the bier: and they that bare him stood still. And he said, **Young man, I say unto thee, Arise.** And he that was dead sat up, and began to speak. And he delivered him to his mother. And there came a fear on all: and they glorified God, saying, That a great prophet is risen up among us; and, That God hath visited his people.
260	*Go your way, and tell John what things ye have seen and heard; how that the blind see, the lame walk, the lepers are cleansed, the deaf hear, the dead are raised, to the poor the gospel is preached.*	Luke 7:20-22 When the men were come unto him, they said, John Baptist hath sent us unto thee, saying, Art thou he that should come? or look we for another? And in that same hour he cured many of their infirmities and plagues, and of evil spirits; and unto many that were blind he gave sight. Then Jesus answering said unto them, **Go your way, and tell John what things ye have seen and heard; how that the blind see, the lame walk, the lepers are cleansed, the deaf hear, the dead are raised, to the poor the gospel is preached.**
261	*Tell me therefore, which of them will love him most?*	Luke 7:40-43 And Jesus answering said unto him, Simon, I have somewhat to say unto thee. And he saith, Master, say on. There was a certain creditor which had two debtors: the one owed five hundred pence, and the other fifty. And when they had nothing to pay, he frankly forgave them both. **Tell me therefore, which of them will love him most?** Simon answered and said, I suppose that he, to whom he forgave most. And he said unto him, Thou hast rightly judged.

Number	Commandment	Context of Commandment

Luke 7:44-50

And he turned to the woman, and said unto Simon, Seest thou this woman? I entered into thine house, thou gavest me no water for my feet: but she hath washed my feet with tears, and wiped them with the hairs of her head. Thou gavest me no kiss: but this woman since the time I came in hath not ceased to kiss my feet.

262   *go in peace.*

My head with oil thou didst not anoint: but this woman hath anointed my feet with ointment. Wherefore I say unto thee, Her sins, which are many, are forgiven; for she loved much: but to whom little is forgiven, the same loveth little. And he said unto her, Thy sins are forgiven. And they that sat at meat with him began to say within themselves, Who is this that forgiveth sins also? And he said to the woman, Thy faith hath saved thee; **go in peace.**

Luke 8:4-8

And when much people were gathered together, and were come to him out of every city, he spake by a parable: A sower went out to sow his seed: and as he sowed, some fell by the way side; and it was trodden down, and the fowls of the air devoured it. And some fell

263   *He that hath ears to hear, let him hear.*

upon a rock; and as soon as it was sprung up, it withered away, because it lacked moisture. And some fell among thorns; and the thorns sprang up with it, and choked it. And other fell on good ground, and sprang up, and bare fruit an hundredfold. And when he had said these things, he cried, **He that hath ears to hear, let him hear.**

Number	Commandment	Context of Commandment
264	*Take heed therefore how ye hear: for whosoever hath, to him shall be given; and whosoever hath not, from him shall be taken even that which he seemeth to have.*	Luke 8:16-18 No man, when he hath lighted a candle, covereth it with a vessel, or putteth it under a bed; but setteth it on a candlestick, that they which enter in may see the light. For nothing is secret, that shall not be made manifest; neither any thing hid, that shall not be known and come abroad. **Take heed therefore how ye hear: for whosoever hath, to him shall be given; and whosoever hath not, from him shall be taken even that which he seemeth to have.**
265	*Let us go over unto the other side of the lake.*	Luke 8:22-24 Now it came to pass on a certain day, that he went into a ship with his disciples: and he said unto them, **Let us go over unto the other side of the lake.** And they launched forth. But as they sailed he fell asleep: and there came down a storm of wind on the lake; and they were filled with water, and were in jeopardy. And they came to him, and awoke him, saying, Master, master, we perish. Then he arose, and rebuked the wind and the raging of the water: and they ceased, and there was a calm.
266	*Return to thine own house, and shew how great things God hath done unto thee.*	Luke 8:38-39 Now the man out of whom the devils were departed besought him that he might be with him: but Jesus sent him away, saying, **Return to thine own house, and shew how great things God hath done unto thee.** And he went his way, and published throughout the whole city how great things Jesus had done unto him.

Number	Commandment	Context of Commandment
267	*Daughter, be of good comfort:*	Luke 8:43-48 And a woman having an issue of blood twelve years, which had spent all her living upon physicians, neither could be healed of any, Came behind him, and touched the border of his garment: and immediately her issue of blood stanched. And Jesus said, Who touched me? When all denied, Peter and they that were with him said, Master, the multitude throng thee and press thee, and sayest thou, Who touched me? And Jesus said, Somebody hath touched me: for I perceive that virtue is gone out of me. And when the woman saw that she was not hid, she came trembling, and falling down before him, she declared unto him before all the people for what cause she had touched him, and how she was healed immediately. And he said unto her, **Daughter, be of good comfort:** thy faith hath made thee whole; go in peace.
268	*Fear not: believe only,*	Luke 8:49-50 While he yet spake, there cometh one from the ruler of the synagogue's house, saying to him, Thy daughter is dead; trouble not the Master. But when Jesus heard it, he answered him, saying, **Fear not: believe only,** and she shall be made whole.
269	*Weep not;*	Luke 8:51-52 And when he came into the house, he suffered no man to go in, save Peter, and James, and John, and the father and the mother of the maiden. And all wept, and bewailed her: but he said, **Weep not;** she is not dead, but sleepeth.
270	*Maid, arise.*	Luke 8:53-56 And they laughed him to scorn, knowing that she was dead. And he put them all out, and took her by the hand, and called, saying, **Maid, arise.** And her spirit came again, and she arose straightway: and he commanded to give her meat. And her parents were astonished: but he charged them that they should tell no man what was done.

Number	Commandment	Context of Commandment
271	*Take nothing for your journey, neither staves, nor scrip, neither bread, neither money; neither have two coats apiece.*	Luke 9:1-3 Then he called his twelve disciples together, and gave them power and authority over all devils, and to cure diseases. And he sent them to preach the kingdom of God, and to heal the sick. And he said unto them, **Take nothing for your journey, neither staves, nor scrip, neither bread, neither money; neither have two coats apiece.**
272	*whatsoever house ye enter into, there abide, and thence depart.*	Luke 9:4 And **whatsoever house ye enter into, there abide, and thence depart.**
273	*whosoever will not receive you, when ye go out of that city, shake off the very dust from your feet for a testimony against them.*	Luke 9:5 And **whosoever will not receive you, when ye go out of that city, shake off the very dust from your feet for a testimony against them.**
274	*Make them sit down by fifties in a company.*	Luke 9:12-14 And when the day began to wear away, then came the twelve, and said unto him, Send the multitude away, that they may go into the towns and country round about, and lodge, and get victuals: for we are here in a desert place. But he said unto them, Give ye them to eat. And they said, We have no more but five loaves and two fishes; except we should go and buy meat for all this people. For they were about five thousand men. And he said to his disciples, **Make them sit down by fifties in a company.**

Number	Commandment	Context of Commandment
275	*If any man will come after me, let him deny himself, and take up his cross daily, and follow me.*	Luke 9:23-24 And he said to them all, **If any man will come after me, let him deny himself, and take up his cross daily, and follow me.** For whosoever will save his life shall lose it: but whosoever will lose his life for my sake, the same shall save it.
276	*Let these sayings sink down into your ears: for the Son of man shall be delivered into the hands of men.*	Luke 9:43-45 And they were all amazed at the mighty power of God. But while they wondered every one at all things which Jesus did, he said unto his disciples, **Let these sayings sink down into your ears: for the Son of man shall be delivered into the hands of men.** But they understood not this saying, and it was hid from them, that they perceived it not: and they feared to ask him of that saying.
277	*Forbid him not: for he that is not against us is for us.*	Luke 9:49-50 And John answered and said, Master, we saw one casting out devils in thy name; and we forbad him, because he followeth not with us. And Jesus said unto him, **Forbid him not: for he that is not against us is for us.**
278	*Follow me.*	Luke 9:57-59 And it came to pass, that, as they went in the way, a certain man said unto him, Lord, I will follow thee whithersoever thou goest. And Jesus said unto him, Foxes have holes, and birds of the air have nests; but the Son of man hath not where to lay his head. And he said unto another, **Follow me.** But he said, Lord, suffer me first to go and bury my father.

Number	Commandment	Context of Commandment
279	*Let the dead bury their dead:*	Luke 9:60 Jesus said unto him, **Let the dead bury their dead:** but go thou and preach the kingdom of God.
280	*go thou and preach the kingdom of God.*	Luke 9:60 Jesus said unto him, Let the dead bury their dead: but **go thou and preach the kingdom of God.**
281	*Go your ways:*	Luke 10:1-3 After these things the Lord appointed other seventy also, and sent them two and two before his face into every city and place, whither he himself would come. Therefore said he unto them, The harvest truly is great, but the labourers are few: pray ye therefore the Lord of the harvest, that he would send forth labourers into his harvest. **Go your ways:** behold, I send you forth as lambs among wolves.
282	*behold, I send you forth as lambs among wolves.*	Luke 10:3 Go your ways: **behold, I send you forth as lambs among wolves.**
283	*Carry neither purse, nor scrip, nor shoes:*	Luke 10:4 **Carry neither purse, nor scrip, nor shoes:** and salute no man by the way.
284	*salute no man by the way.*	Luke 10:4 Carry neither purse, nor scrip, nor shoes: and **salute no man by the way.**
285	*into whatsoever house ye enter, first say, Peace be to this house.*	Luke 10:5-6 And **into whatsoever house ye enter, first say, Peace be to this house.** And if the son of peace be there, your peace shall rest upon it: if not, it shall turn to you again.

Number	Commandment	Context of Commandment
286	*in the same house remain, eating and drinking such things as they give:*	Luke 10:7 And **in the same house remain, eating and drinking such things as they give:** for the labourer is worthy of his hire. Go not from house to house.
287	*Go not from house to house.*	Luke 10:7 And in the same house remain, eating and drinking such things as they give: for the labourer is worthy of his hire. **Go not from house to house.**
288	*into whatsoever city ye enter, and they receive you, eat such things as are set before you:*	Luke 10:8 And **into whatsoever city ye enter, and they receive you, eat such things as are set before you:**
289	*heal the sick that are therein,*	Luke 10:9 And **heal the sick that are therein,** and say unto them, The kingdom of God is come nigh unto you.
290	*say unto them, The kingdom of God is come nigh unto you.*	Luke 10:9 And heal the sick that are therein, and **say unto them, The kingdom of God is come nigh unto you.**

Number	Commandment	Context of Commandment
291	*into whatsoever city ye enter, and they receive you not, go your ways out into the streets of the same, and say, Even the very dust of your city, which cleaveth on us, we do wipe off against you: notwithstanding be ye sure of this, that the kingdom of God is come nigh unto you.*	Luke 10:10-11 But **into whatsoever city ye enter, and they receive you not, go your ways out into the streets of the same, and say, Even the very dust of your city, which cleaveth on us, we do wipe off against you: notwithstanding be ye sure of this, that the kingdom of God is come nigh unto you.**
292	*Behold, I give unto you power to tread on serpents and scorpions, and over all the power of the enemy: and nothing shall by any means hurt you.*	Luke 10:17-19 And the seventy returned again with joy, saying, Lord, even the devils are subject unto us through thy name. And he said unto them, I beheld Satan as lightning fall from heaven. **Behold, I give unto you power to tread on serpents and scorpions, and over all the power of the enemy: and nothing shall by any means hurt you.**
293	*rejoice not, that the spirits are subject unto you;*	Luke 10:20 Notwithstanding in this **rejoice not, that the spirits are subject unto you;** but rather rejoice, because your names are written in heaven.

Number	Commandment	Context of Commandment
294	*rejoice, because your names are written in heaven.*	Luke 10:20 Notwithstanding in this rejoice not, that the spirits are subject unto you; but rather **rejoice, because your names are written in heaven.**
295	*Thou hast answered right: this do, and thou shalt live.*	Luke 10:25-28 And, behold, a certain lawyer stood up, and tempted him, saying, Master, what shall I do to inherit eternal life? He said unto him, What is written in the law? how readest thou? And he answering said, Thou shalt love the Lord thy God with all thy heart, and with all thy soul, and with all thy strength, and with all thy mind; and thy neighbour as thyself. And he said unto him, **Thou hast answered right: this do, and thou shalt live.**
296	*Go, and do thou likewise.*	Luke 10:29-37 But he, willing to justify himself, said unto Jesus, And who is my neighbour? And Jesus answering said, A certain man went down from Jerusalem to Jericho, and fell among thieves, which stripped him of his raiment, and wounded him, and departed, leaving him half dead. And by chance there came down a certain priest that way: and when he saw him, he passed by on the other side. And likewise a Levite, when he was at the place, came and looked on him, and passed by on the other side. But a certain Samaritan, as he journeyed, came where he was: and when he saw him, he had compassion on him, And went to him, and bound up his wounds, pouring in oil and wine, and set him on his own beast, and brought him to an inn, and took care of him. And on the morrow when he departed, he took out two pence, and gave them to the host, and said unto him, Take care of him; and whatsoever thou spendest more, when I come again, I will repay thee. Which now of these three, thinkest thou, was neighbour unto him that fell among the thieves? And he said, He that shewed mercy on him. Then said Jesus unto him, **Go, and do thou likewise.**

Number	Commandment	Context of Commandment
297	*Take heed therefore that the light which is in thee be not darkness.*	Luke 11:33-36 No man, when he hath lighted a candle, putteth it in a secret place, neither under a bushel, but on a candlestick, that they which come in may see the light. The light of the body is the eye: therefore when thine eye is single, thy whole body also is full of light; but when thine eye is evil, thy body also is full of darkness. **Take heed therefore that the light which is in thee be not darkness.** If thy whole body therefore be full of light, having no part dark, the whole shall be full of light, as when the bright shining of a candle doth give thee light.
298	*give alms of such things as ye have; and, behold, all things are clean unto you.*	Luke 11:37-42 And as he spake, a certain Pharisee besought him to dine with him: and he went in, and sat down to meat. And when the Pharisee saw it, he marvelled that he had not first washed before dinner. And the Lord said unto him, Now do ye Pharisees make clean the outside of the cup and the platter; but your inward part is full of ravening and wickedness. Ye fools, did not he that made that which is without make that which is within also? But rather **give alms of such things as ye have; and, behold, all things are clean unto you.** But woe unto you, Pharisees! for ye tithe mint and rue and all manner of herbs, and pass over judgment and the love of God: these ought ye to have done, and not to leave the other undone.
299	*Beware ye of the leaven of the Pharisees, which is hypocrisy.*	Luke 12:1-3 In the mean time, when there were gathered together an innumerable multitude of people, insomuch that they trode one upon another, he began to say unto his disciples first of all, **Beware ye of the leaven of the Pharisees, which is hypocrisy.** For there is nothing covered, that shall not be revealed; neither hid, that shall not be known. Therefore whatsoever ye have spoken in darkness shall be heard in the light; and that which ye have spoken in the ear in closets shall be proclaimed upon the housetops.

Number	Commandment	Context of Commandment
300	*Be not afraid of them that kill the body, and after that have no more that they can do.*	Luke 12:4 And I say unto you my friends, **Be not afraid of them that kill the body, and after that have no more that they can do.**
301	*Fear him, which after he hath killed hath power to cast into hell;*	Luke 12:5 But I will forewarn you whom ye shall fear: **Fear him, which after he hath killed hath power to cast into hell;** yea, I say unto you, Fear him.
302	*Fear him.*	Luke 12:5 But I will forewarn you whom ye shall fear: Fear him, which after he hath killed hath power to cast into hell; yea, I say unto you, **Fear him.**
303	*take ye no thought how or what thing ye shall answer, or what ye shall say:*	Luke 12:11-12 And when they bring you unto the synagogues, and unto magistrates, and powers, **take ye no thought how or what thing ye shall answer, or what ye shall say:** For the Holy Ghost shall teach you in the same hour what ye ought to say.
304	*Take heed, and beware of covetousness:*	Luke 12:13-15 And one of the company said unto him, Master, speak to my brother, that he divide the inheritance with me. And he said unto him, Man, who made me a judge or a divider over you? And he said unto them, **Take heed, and beware of covetousness:** for a man's life consisteth not in the abundance of the things which he possesseth.

Number	Commandment	Context of Commandment
305	*Consider the ravens: for they neither sow nor reap; which neither have storehouse nor barn; and God feedeth them:*	Luke 12:22-24 And he said unto his disciples, Therefore I say unto you, Take no thought for your life, what ye shall eat; neither for the body, what ye shall put on. The life is more than meat, and the body is more than raiment. **Consider the ravens: for they neither sow nor reap; which neither have storehouse nor barn; and God feedeth them:** how much more are ye better than the fowls?
306	*seek not ye what ye shall eat, or what ye shall drink,*	Luke 12:29 And **seek not ye what ye shall eat, or what ye shall drink,** neither be ye of doubtful mind.
307	*neither be ye of doubtful mind.*	Luke 12:29-30 And seek not ye what ye shall eat, or what ye shall drink, **neither be ye of doubtful mind.** For all these things do the nations of the world seek after: and your Father knoweth that ye have need of these things.
308	*seek ye the kingdom of God;*	Luke 12:31 But rather **seek ye the kingdom of God;** and all these things shall be added unto you.
309	*Fear not, little flock; for it is your Father's good pleasure to give you the kingdom.*	Luke 12:32 **Fear not, little flock; for it is your Father's good pleasure to give you the kingdom.**

Number	Commandment	Context of Commandment
310	*Sell that ye have, and give alms; provide yourselves bags which wax not old, a treasure in the heavens that faileth not, where no thief approacheth, neither moth corrupteth.*	**Luke 12:33-34** **Sell that ye have, and give alms; provide yourselves bags which wax not old, a treasure in the heavens that faileth not, where no thief approacheth, neither moth corrupteth.** For where your treasure is, there will your heart be also.
311	*Let your loins be girded about, and your lights burning; And ye yourselves like unto men that wait for their lord, when he will return from the wedding; that when he cometh and knocketh, they may open unto him immediately.*	Luke 12:35-37 **Let your loins be girded about, and your lights burning; And ye yourselves like unto men that wait for their lord, when he will return from the wedding; that when he cometh and knocketh, they may open unto him immediately.** Blessed are those servants, whom the lord when he cometh shall find watching: verily I say unto you, that he shall gird himself, and make them to sit down to meat, and will come forth and serve them.

Number	Commandment	Context of Commandment
312	*When thou goest with thine adversary to the magistrate, as thou art in the way, give diligence that thou mayest be delivered from him; lest he hale thee to the judge, and the judge deliver thee to the officer, and the officer cast thee into prison.*	Luke 12:58-59 **When thou goest with thine adversary to the magistrate, as thou art in the way, give diligence that thou mayest be delivered from him; lest he hale thee to the judge, and the judge deliver thee to the officer, and the officer cast thee into prison.** I tell thee, thou shalt not depart thence, till thou hast paid the very last mite.
313	*Strive to enter in at the strait gate: for many, I say unto you, will seek to enter in, and shall not be able.*	Luke 13:23-24 Then said one unto him, Lord, are there few that be saved? And he said unto them, **Strive to enter in at the strait gate: for many, I say unto you, will seek to enter in, and shall not be able.**
314	*behold, there are last which shall be first, and there are first which shall be last.*	Luke 13:28-30 There shall be weeping and gnashing of teeth, when ye shall see Abraham, and Isaac, and Jacob, and all the prophets, in the kingdom of God, and you yourselves thrust out. And they shall come from the east, and from the west, and from the north, and from the south, and shall sit down in the kingdom of God. And, **behold, there are last which shall be first, and there are first which shall be last.**

Number	Commandment	Context of Commandment
315	*Go ye, and tell that fox, Behold, I cast out devils, and I do cures to day and to morrow, and the third day I shall be perfected. Nevertheless I must walk to day, and to morrow, and the day following: for it cannot be that a prophet perish out of Jerusalem.*	Luke 13:31-33 The same day there came certain of the Pharisees, saying unto him, Get thee out, and depart hence: for Herod will kill thee. And he said unto them, **Go ye, and tell that fox, Behold, I cast out devils, and I do cures to day and to morrow, and the third day I shall be perfected. Nevertheless I must walk to day, and to morrow, and the day following: for it cannot be that a prophet perish out of Jerusalem.**
316	*When thou art bidden of any man to a wedding, sit not down in the highest room;*	Luke 14:8-9 **When thou art bidden of any man to a wedding, sit not down in the highest room;** lest a more honourable man than thou be bidden of him; And he that bade thee and him come and say to thee, Give this man place; and thou begin with shame to take the lowest room.
317	*when thou art bidden, go and sit down in the lowest room;*	Luke 14:10-11 But **when thou art bidden, go and sit down in the lowest room;** that when he that bade thee cometh, he may say unto thee, Friend, go up higher: then shalt thou have worship in the presence of them that sit at meat with thee. For whosoever exalteth himself shall be abased; and he that humbleth himself shall be exalted.

Number	Commandment	Context of Commandment
318	*When thou makest a dinner or a supper, call not thy friends, nor thy brethren, neither thy kinsmen, nor thy rich neighbours;*	Luke 14:12 Then said he also to him that bade him, **When thou makest a dinner or a supper, call not thy friends, nor thy brethren, neither thy kinsmen, nor thy rich neighbours;** lest they also bid thee again, and a recompence be made thee.
319	*when thou makest a feast, call the poor, the maimed, the lame, the blind:*	Luke 14:13-14 But **when thou makest a feast, call the poor, the maimed, the lame, the blind:** And thou shalt be blessed; for they cannot recompense thee: for thou shalt be recompensed at the resurrection of the just.
320	*He that hath ears to hear, let him hear.*	Luke 14:25-35 And there went great multitudes with him: and he turned, and said unto them, If any man come to me, and hate not his father, and mother, and wife, and children, and brethren, and sisters, yea, and his own life also, he cannot be my disciple. And whosoever doth not bear his cross, and come after me, cannot be my disciple. For which of you, intending to build a tower, sitteth not down first, and counteth the cost, whether he have sufficient to finish it? Lest haply, after he hath laid the foundation, and is not able to finish it, all that behold it begin to mock him, Saying, This man began to build, and was not able to finish. Or what king, going to make war against another king, sitteth not down first, and consulteth whether he be able with ten thousand to meet him that cometh against him with twenty thousand? Or else, while the other is yet a great way off, he sendeth an ambassage, and desireth conditions of peace. So likewise, whosoever he be of you that forsaketh not all that he hath, he cannot be my disciple. Salt is good: but if the salt have lost his savour, wherewith shall it be seasoned? It is neither fit for the land, nor yet for the dunghill; but men cast it out. **He that hath ears to hear, let him hear.**

Number	Commandment	Context of Commandment

Luke 16:1-13

And he said also unto his disciples, There was a certain rich man, which had a steward; and the same was accused unto him that he had wasted his goods. And he called him, and said unto him, How is it that I hear this of thee? give an account of thy stewardship; for thou mayest be no longer steward. Then the steward said within himself, What shall I do? for my lord taketh away from me the stewardship: I cannot dig; to beg I am ashamed. I am resolved what to do, that, when I am put out of the stewardship, they may receive me into their houses. So he called every one of his lord's debtors unto him, and said unto the first, How much owest thou unto my lord? And he said, An hundred measures of oil. And he said unto him, Take thy bill, and sit down quickly, and write fifty. Then said he to another, And how much owest thou? And he said, An hundred measures of wheat. And he said unto him, Take thy bill, and write fourscore. And the lord commended the unjust steward, because he had done wisely: for the children of this world are in their generation wiser than the children of light. And I say unto you, **Make to yourselves friends of the mammon of unrighteousness; that, when ye fail, they may receive you into everlasting habitations.** He that is faithful in that which is least is faithful also in much: and he that is unjust in the least is unjust also in much. If therefore ye have not been faithful in the unrighteous mammon, who will commit to your trust the true riches? And if ye have not been faithful in that which is another man's, who shall give you that which is your own? No servant can serve two masters: for either he will hate the one, and love the other; or else he will hold to the one, and despise the other. Ye cannot serve God and mammon.

321 — *Make to yourselves friends of the mammon of unrighteousness; that, when ye fail, they may receive you into everlasting habitations.*

Number	Commandment	Context of Commandment
322	*Take heed to yourselves:*	Luke 17:3 **Take heed to yourselves:** If thy brother trespass against thee, rebuke him; and if he repent, forgive him.
323	*If thy brother trespass against thee, rebuke him;*	Luke 17:3 Take heed to yourselves: **If thy brother trespass against thee, rebuke him;** and if he repent, forgive him.
324	*if he repent, forgive him.*	Luke 17:3 Take heed to yourselves: If thy brother trespass against thee, rebuke him; and **if he repent, forgive him.**
325	*if he trespass against thee seven times in a day, and seven times in a day turn again to thee, saying, I repent; thou shalt forgive him.*	Luke 17:4 And **if he trespass against thee seven times in a day, and seven times in a day turn again to thee, saying, I repent; thou shalt forgive him.**
326	*when ye shall have done all those things which are commanded you, say, We are unprofitable servants: we have done that which was our duty to do.*	Luke 17:7-10 But which of you, having a servant plowing or feeding cattle, will say unto him by and by, when he is come from the field, Go and sit down to meat? And will not rather say unto him, Make ready wherewith I may sup, and gird thyself, and serve me, till I have eaten and drunken; and afterward thou shalt eat and drink? Doth he thank that servant because he did the things that were commanded him? I trow not. So likewise ye, **when ye shall have done all those things which are commanded you, say, We are unprofitable servants: we have done that which was our duty to do.**

Commandments of Jesus Christ found in: The Gospel According To Luke

Number	Commandment	Context of Commandment
327	*Go shew yourselves unto the priests.*	Luke 17:12-14 And as he entered into a certain village, there met him ten men that were lepers, which stood afar off: And they lifted up their voices, and said, Jesus, Master, have mercy on us. And when he saw them, he said unto them, **Go shew yourselves unto the priests.** And it came to pass, that, as they went, they were cleansed.
328	*Arise, go thy way: thy faith hath made thee whole.*	Luke 17:15-19 And one of them, when he saw that he was healed, turned back, and with a loud voice glorified God, And fell down on his face at his feet, giving him thanks: and he was a Samaritan. And Jesus answering said, Were there not ten cleansed? but where are the nine? There are not found that returned to give glory to God, save this stranger. And he said unto him, **Arise, go thy way: thy faith hath made thee whole.**
329	*behold, the kingdom of God is within you.*	Luke 17:20-21 And when he was demanded of the Pharisees, when the kingdom of God should come, he answered them and said, The kingdom of God cometh not with observation: Neither shall they say, Lo here! or, lo there! for, **behold, the kingdom of God is within you.**
330	*The days will come, when ye shall desire to see one of the days of the Son of man, and ye shall not see it. And they shall say to you, See here; or, see there: go not after them, nor follow them.*	Luke 17:20-24 And when he was demanded of the Pharisees, when the kingdom of God should come, he answered them and said, The kingdom of God cometh not with observation: Neither shall they say, Lo here! or, lo there! for, behold, the kingdom of God is within you. And he said unto the disciples, **The days will come, when ye shall desire to see one of the days of the Son of man, and ye shall not see it. And they shall say to you, See here; or, see there: go not after them, nor follow them.** For as the lightning, that lighteneth out of the one part under heaven, shineth unto the other part under heaven; so shall also the Son of man be in his day.

Number	Commandment	Context of Commandment
331	*In that day, he which shall be upon the housetop, and his stuff in the house, let him not come down to take it away:*	Luke 17:26-31 And as it was in the days of Noe, so shall it be also in the days of the Son of man. They did eat, they drank, they married wives, they were given in marriage, until the day that Noah entered into the ark, and the flood came, and destroyed them all. Likewise also as it was in the days of Lot; they did eat, they drank, they bought, they sold, they planted, they builded; But the same day that Lot went out of Sodom it rained fire and brimstone from heaven, and destroyed them all. Even thus shall it be in the day when the Son of man is revealed. **In that day, he which shall be upon the housetop, and his stuff in the house, let him not come down to take it away:** and he that is in the field, let him likewise not return back.
332	*he that is in the field, let him likewise not return back.*	Luke 17:31 In that day, he which shall be upon the housetop, and his stuff in the house, let him not come down to take it away: and **he that is in the field, let him likewise not return back.**
333	*Remember Lot's wife.*	Luke 17:32-33 **Remember Lot's wife.** Whosoever shall seek to save his life shall lose it; and whosoever shall lose his life shall preserve it.

Number	Commandment	Context of Commandment
334	*Hear what the unjust judge saith.*	Luke 18:1-8 And he spake a parable unto them to this end, that men ought always to pray, and not to faint; Saying, There was in a city a judge, which feared not God, neither regarded man: And there was a widow in that city; and she came unto him, saying, Avenge me of mine adversary. And he would not for a while: but afterward he said within himself, Though I fear not God, nor regard man; Yet because this widow troubleth me, I will avenge her, lest by her continual coming she weary me. And the Lord said, **Hear what the unjust judge saith.** And shall not God avenge his own elect, which cry day and night unto him, though he bear long with them? I tell you that he will avenge them speedily. Nevertheless when the Son of man cometh, shall he find faith on the earth?
335	*Suffer little children to come unto me, and forbid them not:*	Luke 18:15-17 And they brought unto him also infants, that he would touch them: but when his disciples saw it, they rebuked them. But Jesus called them unto him, and said, **Suffer little children to come unto me, and forbid them not:** for of such is the kingdom of God. Verily I say unto you, Whosoever shall not receive the kingdom of God as a little child shall in no wise enter therein.
336	*sell all that thou hast, and distribute unto the poor, and thou shalt have treasure in heaven: and come, follow me.*	Luke 18:18-22 And a certain ruler asked him, saying, Good Master, what shall I do to inherit eternal life? And Jesus said unto him, Why callest thou me good? none is good, save one, that is, God. Thou knowest the commandments, Do not commit adultery, Do not kill, Do not steal, Do not bear false witness, Honour thy father and thy mother. And he said, All these have I kept from my youth up. Now when Jesus heard these things, he said unto him, Yet lackest thou one thing: **sell all that thou hast, and distribute unto the poor, and thou shalt have treasure in heaven: and come, follow me.**

Number	Commandment	Context of Commandment

Behold, we go up to Jerusalem, and all things that are written by the prophets concerning the Son of man shall be accomplished. For he shall be delivered unto the Gentiles, and shall be mocked, and spitefully entreated, and spitted on: And they shall scourge him, and put him to death: and the third day he shall rise again.

337

Luke 18:31-33
Then he took unto him the twelve, and said unto them, **Behold, we go up to Jerusalem, and all things that are written by the prophets concerning the Son of man shall be accomplished. For he shall be delivered unto the Gentiles, and shall be mocked, and spitefully entreated, and spitted on: And they shall scourge him, and put him to death: and the third day he shall rise again.**

338

Receive thy sight: thy faith hath saved thee.

Luke 18:35-43
And it came to pass, that as he was come nigh unto Jericho, a certain blind man sat by the way side begging: And hearing the multitude pass by, he asked what it meant. And they told him, that Jesus of Nazareth passeth by. And he cried, saying, Jesus, thou son of David, have mercy on me. And they which went before rebuked him, that he should hold his peace: but he cried so much the more, Thou son of David, have mercy on me. And Jesus stood, and commanded him to be brought unto him: and when he was come near, he asked him, Saying, What wilt thou that I shall do unto thee? And he said, Lord, that I may receive my sight. And Jesus said unto him, **Receive thy sight: thy faith hath saved thee.** And immediately he received his sight, and followed him, glorifying God: and all the people, when they saw it, gave praise unto God.

Number	Commandment	Context of Commandment
339	*Zacchaeus, make haste, and come down; for to day I must abide at thy house.*	Luke 19:1-6 And Jesus entered and passed through Jericho. And, behold, there was a man named Zacchaeus, which was the chief among the publicans, and he was rich. And he sought to see Jesus who he was; and could not for the press, because he was little of stature. And he ran before, and climbed up into a sycomore tree to see him: for he was to pass that way. And when Jesus came to the place, he looked up, and saw him, and said unto him, **Zacchaeus, make haste, and come down; for to day I must abide at thy house.** And he made haste, and came down, and received him joyfully.
340	*if any man ask you, Why do ye loose him? thus shall ye say unto him, Because the Lord hath need of him.*	Luke 19:29-31 And it came to pass, when he was come nigh to Bethphage and Bethany, at the mount called the mount of Olives, he sent two of his disciples, Saying, Go ye into the village over against you; in the which at your entering ye shall find a colt tied, whereon yet never man sat: loose him, and bring him hither. And **if any man ask you, Why do ye loose him? thus shall ye say unto him, Because the Lord hath need of him.**
341	*Shew me a penny.*	Luke 20:21-25 And they asked him, saying, Master, we know that thou sayest and teachest rightly, neither acceptest thou the person of any, but teachest the way of God truly: Is it lawful for us to give tribute unto Caesar, or no? But he perceived their craftiness, and said unto them, Why tempt ye me? **Shew me a penny.** Whose image and superscription hath it? They answered and said, Caesar's. And he said unto them, Render therefore unto Caesar the things which be Caesar's, and unto God the things which be God's.

Number	Commandment	Context of Commandment
342	*Beware of the scribes, which desire to walk in long robes, and love greetings in the markets, and the highest seats in the synagogues, and the chief rooms at feasts; Which devour widows' houses, and for a shew make long prayers: the same shall receive greater damnation.*	Luke 20:45-47 Then in the audience of all the people he said unto his disciples, **Beware of the scribes, which desire to walk in long robes, and love greetings in the markets, and the highest seats in the synagogues, and the chief rooms at feasts; Which devour widows' houses, and for a shew make long prayers: the same shall receive greater damnation.**
343	*Take heed that ye be not deceived:*	Luke 21:5-8 And as some spake of the temple, how it was adorned with goodly stones and gifts, he said, As for these things which ye behold, the days will come, in the which there shall not be left one stone upon another, that shall not be thrown down. And they asked him, saying, Master, but when shall these things be? and what sign will there be when these things shall come to pass? And he said, **Take heed that ye be not deceived:** for many shall come in my name, saying, I am Christ; and the time draweth near: go ye not therefore after them.

Number	Commandment	Context of Commandment
344	*go ye not therefore after them.*	Luke 21:8 And he said, Take heed that ye be not deceived: for many shall come in my name, saying, I am Christ; and the time draweth near: **go ye not therefore after them.**
345	*when ye shall hear of wars and commotions, be not terrified:*	Luke 21:9 But **when ye shall hear of wars and commotions, be not terrified:** for these things must first come to pass; but the end is not by and by.
346	*Settle it therefore in your hearts, not to meditate before what ye shall answer:*	Luke 21:10-15 Then said he unto them, Nation shall rise against nation, and kingdom against kingdom: And great earthquakes shall be in divers places, and famines, and pestilences; and fearful sights and great signs shall there be from heaven. But before all these, they shall lay their hands on you, and persecute you, delivering you up to the synagogues, and into prisons, being brought before kings and rulers for my name's sake. And it shall turn to you for a testimony. **Settle it therefore in your hearts, not to meditate before what ye shall answer:** For I will give you a mouth and wisdom, which all your adversaries shall not be able to gainsay nor resist.
347	*when ye shall see Jerusalem compassed with armies, then know that the desolation thereof is nigh.*	Luke 21:20 And **when ye shall see Jerusalem compassed with armies, then know that the desolation thereof is nigh.**

Number	Commandment	Context of Commandment
348	*let them which are in Judaea flee to the mountains;*	Luke 21:21 Then **let them which are in Judaea flee to the mountains;** and let them which are in the midst of it depart out; and let not them that are in the countries enter thereinto.
349	*let them which are in the midst of it depart out;*	Luke 21:21 Then let them which are in Judaea flee to the mountains; and **let them which are in the midst of it depart out;** and let not them that are in the countries enter thereinto.
350	*let not them that are in the countries enter thereinto.*	Luke 21:21-22 Then let them which are in Judaea flee to the mountains; and let them which are in the midst of it depart out; and **let not them that are in the countries enter thereinto.** For these be the days of vengeance, that all things which are written may be fulfilled.
351	*when these things begin to come to pass, then look up, and lift up your heads; for your redemption draweth nigh.*	Luke 21:23-28 But woe unto them that are with child, and to them that give suck, in those days! for there shall be great distress in the land, and wrath upon this people. And they shall fall by the edge of the sword, and shall be led away captive into all nations: and Jerusalem shall be trodden down of the Gentiles, until the times of the Gentiles be fulfilled. And there shall be signs in the sun, and in the moon, and in the stars; and upon the earth distress of nations, with perplexity; the sea and the waves roaring; Men's hearts failing them for fear, and for looking after those things which are coming on the earth: for the powers of heaven shall be shaken. And then shall they see the Son of man coming in a cloud with power and great glory. And **when these things begin to come to pass, then look up, and lift up your heads; for your redemption draweth nigh.**

Number	Commandment	Context of Commandment
352	*Behold the fig tree, and all the trees;*	Luke 21:29-30 And he spake to them a parable; **Behold the fig tree, and all the trees;** When they now shoot forth, ye see and know of your own selves that summer is now nigh at hand.
353	*So likewise ye, when ye see these things come to pass, know ye that the kingdom of God is nigh at hand.*	Luke 21:31 **So likewise ye, when ye see these things come to pass, know ye that the kingdom of God is nigh at hand.**
354	*take heed to yourselves, lest at any time your hearts be overcharged with surfeiting, and drunkenness, and cares of this life, and so that day come upon you unawares.*	Luke 21:32-35 Verily I say unto you, This generation shall not pass away, till all be fulfilled. Heaven and earth shall pass away: but my words shall not pass away. And **take heed to yourselves, lest at any time your hearts be overcharged with surfeiting, and drunkenness, and cares of this life, and so that day come upon you unawares.** For as a snare shall it come on all them that dwell on the face of the whole earth.
355	*Watch ye therefore, and pray always, that ye may be accounted worthy to escape all these things that shall come to pass, and to stand before the Son of man.*	Luke 21:36 **Watch ye therefore, and pray always, that ye may be accounted worthy to escape all these things that shall come to pass, and to stand before the Son of man.**

Number	Commandment	Context of Commandment
356	*Go and prepare us the passover, that we may eat.*	Luke 22:7-8 Then came the day of unleavened bread, when the passover must be killed. And he sent Peter and John, saying, **Go and prepare us the passover, that we may eat.**
357	*Behold, when ye are entered into the city, there shall a man meet you, bearing a pitcher of water; follow him into the house where he entereth in.*	Luke 22:9-10 And they said unto him, Where wilt thou that we prepare? And he said unto them, **Behold, when ye are entered into the city, there shall a man meet you, bearing a pitcher of water; follow him into the house where he entereth in.**
358	*say unto the goodman of the house, The Master saith unto thee, Where is the guestchamber, where I shall eat the passover with my disciples?*	Luke 22:11 And ye shall **say unto the goodman of the house, The Master saith unto thee, Where is the guestchamber, where I shall eat the passover with my disciples?**
359	*there make ready.*	Luke 22:12 And he shall shew you a large upper room furnished: **there make ready.**

Number	Commandment	Context of Commandment
360	*Take this, and divide it among yourselves:*	Luke 22:13-18 And they went, and found as he had said unto them: and they made ready the passover. And when the hour was come, he sat down, and the twelve apostles with him. And he said unto them, With desire I have desired to eat this passover with you before I suffer: For I say unto you, I will not any more eat thereof, until it be fulfilled in the kingdom of God. And he took the cup, and gave thanks, and said, **Take this, and divide it among yourselves:** For I say unto you, I will not drink of the fruit of the vine, until the kingdom of God shall come.
361	*this do in remembrance of me.*	Luke 22:19 And he took bread, and gave thanks, and brake it, and gave unto them, saying, This is my body which is given for you: **this do in remembrance of me.**
362	*behold, the hand of him that betrayeth me is with me on the table.*	Luke 22:21-22 But, **behold, the hand of him that betrayeth me is with me on the table.** And truly the Son of man goeth, as it was determined: but woe unto that man by whom he is betrayed!
363	*he that is greatest among you, let him be as the younger; and he that is chief, as he that doth serve.*	Luke 22:24-27 And there was also a strife among them, which of them should be accounted the greatest. And he said unto them, The kings of the Gentiles exercise lordship over them; and they that exercise authority upon them are called benefactors. But ye shall not be so: but **he that is greatest among you, let him be as the younger; and he that is chief, as he that doth serve.** For whether is greater, he that sitteth at meat, or he that serveth? is not he that sitteth at meat? but I am among you as he that serveth.

Number	Commandment	Context of Commandment
364	*behold, Satan hath desired to have you, that he may sift you as wheat:*	Luke 22:31 And the Lord said, Simon, Simon, **behold, Satan hath desired to have you, that he may sift you as wheat:**
365	*when thou art converted, strengthen thy brethren.*	Luke 22:32 But I have prayed for thee, that thy faith fail not: and **when thou art converted, strengthen thy brethren.**
366	*he that hath a purse, let him take it, and likewise his scrip: and he that hath no sword, let him sell his garment, and buy one.*	Luke 22:35-37 And he said unto them, When I sent you without purse, and scrip, and shoes, lacked ye any thing? And they said, Nothing. Then said he unto them, But now, **he that hath a purse, let him take it, and likewise his scrip: and he that hath no sword, let him sell his garment, and buy one.** For I say unto you, that this that is written must yet be accomplished in me, And he was reckoned among the transgressors: for the things concerning me have an end.
367	*Father, if thou be willing, remove this cup from me: nevertheless not my will, but thine, be done.*	Luke 22:40-42 And when he was at the place, he said unto them, Pray that ye enter not into temptation. And he was withdrawn from them about a stone's cast, and kneeled down, and prayed, Saying, **Father, if thou be willing, remove this cup from me: nevertheless not my will, but thine, be done.**
368	*rise and pray, lest ye enter into temptation.*	Luke 22:43-46 And there appeared an angel unto him from heaven, strengthening him. And being in an agony he prayed more earnestly: and his sweat was as it were great drops of blood falling down to the ground. And when he rose up from prayer, and was come to his disciples, he found them sleeping for sorrow, And said unto them, Why sleep ye? **rise and pray, lest ye enter into temptation.**

Number	Commandment	Context of Commandment
369	*Suffer ye thus far.*	Luke 22:47-51 And while he yet spake, behold a multitude, and he that was called Judas, one of the twelve, went before them, and drew near unto Jesus to kiss him. But Jesus said unto him, Judas, betrayest thou the Son of man with a kiss? When they which were about him saw what would follow, they said unto him, Lord, shall we smite with the sword? And one of them smote the servant of the high priest, and cut off his right ear. And Jesus answered and said, **Suffer ye thus far.** And he touched his ear, and healed him.
370	*Daughters of Jerusalem, weep not for me, but weep for yourselves, and for your children.*	Luke 23:26-28 And as they led him away, they laid hold upon one Simon, a Cyrenian, coming out of the country, and on him they laid the cross, that he might bear it after Jesus. And there followed him a great company of people, and of women, which also bewailed and lamented him. But Jesus turning unto them said, **Daughters of Jerusalem, weep not for me, but weep for yourselves, and for your children.**
371	*behold, the days are coming, in the which they shall say, Blessed are the barren, and the wombs that never bare, and the paps which never gave suck.*	Luke 23:29-31 For, **behold, the days are coming, in the which they shall say, Blessed are the barren, and the wombs that never bare, and the paps which never gave suck.** Then shall they begin to say to the mountains, Fall on us; and to the hills, Cover us. For if they do these things in a green tree, what shall be done in the dry?

Number	Commandment	Context of Commandment
372	*Father, forgive them; for they know not what they do.*	Luke 23:32-34 And there were also two other, malefactors, led with him to be put to death. And when they were come to the place, which is called Calvary, there they crucified him, and the malefactors, one on the right hand, and the other on the left. Then said Jesus, **Father, forgive them; for they know not what they do.** And they parted his raiment, and cast lots.
373	*Behold my hands and my feet, that it is I myself: handle me, and see;*	Luke 24:36-40 And as they thus spake, Jesus himself stood in the midst of them, and saith unto them, Peace be unto you. But they were terrified and affrighted, and supposed that they had seen a spirit. And he said unto them, Why are ye troubled? and why do thoughts arise in your hearts? **Behold my hands and my feet, that it is I myself: handle me, and see;** for a spirit hath not flesh and bones, as ye see me have. And when he had thus spoken, he shewed them his hands and his feet.
374	*behold, I send the promise of my Father upon you:*	Luke 24:45-49 Then opened he their understanding, that they might understand the scriptures, And said unto them, Thus it is written, and thus it behooved Christ to suffer, and to rise from the dead the third day: And that repentance and remission of sins should be preached in his name among all nations, beginning at Jerusalem. And ye are witnesses of these things. And, **behold, I send the promise of my Father upon you:** but tarry ye in the city of Jerusalem, until ye be endued with power from on high.
375	*tarry ye in the city of Jerusalem, until ye be endued with power from on high.*	Luke 24:49 And, behold, I send the promise of my Father upon you: but **tarry ye in the city of Jerusalem, until ye be endued with power from on high.**

Commandments of Jesus Christ found in:

THE GOSPEL ACCORDING TO JOHN

Number	Commandment	Context of Commandment
376	*Come and see.*	John 1:35-39 Again the next day after John stood, and two of his disciples; And looking upon Jesus as he walked, he saith, Behold the Lamb of God! And the two disciples heard him speak, and they followed Jesus. Then Jesus turned, and saw them following, and saith unto them, What seek ye? They said unto him, Rabbi, (which is to say, being interpreted, Master,) where dwellest thou? He saith unto them, **Come and see.** They came and saw where he dwelt, and abode with him that day: for it was about the tenth hour.
377	*Follow me.*	John 1:43-44 The day following Jesus would go forth into Galilee, and findeth Philip, and saith unto him, **Follow me.** Now Philip was of Bethsaida, the city of Andrew and Peter.
378	*Behold an Israelite indeed, in whom is no guile!*	John 1:45-51 Philip findeth Nathanael, and saith unto him, We have found him, of whom Moses in the law, and the prophets, did write, Jesus of Nazareth, the son of Joseph. And Nathanael said unto him, Can there any good thing come out of Nazareth? Philip saith unto him, Come and see. Jesus saw Nathanael coming to him, and saith of him, **Behold an Israelite indeed, in whom is no guile!** Nathanael saith unto him, Whence knowest thou me? Jesus answered and said unto him, Before that Philip called thee, when thou wast under the fig tree, I saw thee. Nathanael answered and saith unto him, Rabbi, thou art the Son of God; thou art the King of Israel. Jesus answered and said unto him, Because I said unto thee, I saw thee under the fig tree, believest thou? thou shalt see greater things than these. And he saith unto him, Verily, verily, I say unto you, Hereafter ye shall see heaven open, and the angels of God ascending and descending upon the Son of man.

Number	Commandment	Context of Commandment
379	*Fill the waterpots with water.*	John 2:1-7 And the third day there was a marriage in Cana of Galilee; and the mother of Jesus was there: And both Jesus was called, and his disciples, to the marriage. And when they wanted wine, the mother of Jesus saith unto him, They have no wine. Jesus saith unto her, Woman, what have I to do with thee? mine hour is not yet come. His mother saith unto the servants, Whatsoever he saith unto you, do it. And there were set there six waterpots of stone, after the manner of the purifying of the Jews, containing two or three firkins apiece. Jesus saith unto them, **Fill the waterpots with water.** And they filled them up to the brim.
380	*Draw out now, and bear unto the governor of the feast.*	John 2:8-11 And he saith unto them, **Draw out now, and bear unto the governor of the feast.** And they bare it. When the ruler of the feast had tasted the water that was made wine, and knew not whence it was: (but the servants which drew the water knew;) the governor of the feast called the bridegroom, And saith unto him, Every man at the beginning doth set forth good wine; and when men have well drunk, then that which is worse: but thou hast kept the good wine until now. This beginning of miracles did Jesus in Cana of Galilee, and manifested forth his glory; and his disciples believed on him.
381	*Take these things hence; make not my Father's house an house of merchandise.*	John 2:13-16 And the Jews' passover was at hand, and Jesus went up to Jerusalem. And found in the temple those that sold oxen and sheep and doves, and the changers of money sitting: And when he had made a scourge of small cords, he drove them all out of the temple, and the sheep, and the oxen; and poured out the changers' money, and overthrew the tables; And said unto them that sold doves, **Take these things hence; make not my Father's house an house of merchandise.**

Number	Commandment	Context of Commandment
382	*Destroy this temple, and in three days I will raise it up.*	John 2:18-22 Then answered the Jews and said unto him, What sign shewest thou unto us, seeing that thou doest these things? Jesus answered and said unto them, **Destroy this temple, and in three days I will raise it up.** Then said the Jews, Forty and six years was this temple in building, and wilt thou rear it up in three days? But he spake of the temple of his body. When therefore he was risen from the dead, his disciples remembered that he had said this unto them; and they believed the scripture, and the word which Jesus had said.
383	*Marvel not that I said unto thee, Ye must be born again.*	John 3:3-8 Jesus answered and said unto him, Verily, verily, I say unto thee, Except a man be born again, he cannot see the kingdom of God. Nicodemus saith unto him, How can a man be born when he is old? can he enter the second time into his mother's womb, and be born? Jesus answered, Verily, verily, I say unto thee, Except a man be born of water and of the Spirit, he cannot enter into the kingdom of God. That which is born of the flesh is flesh; and that which is born of the Spirit is spirit. **Marvel not that I said unto thee, Ye must be born again.** The wind bloweth where it listeth, and thou hearest the sound thereof, but canst not tell whence it cometh, and whither it goeth: so is every one that is born of the Spirit.
384	*Give me to drink.*	John 4:3-7 He left Judaea, and departed again into Galilee. And he must needs go through Samaria. Then cometh he to a city of Samaria, which is called Sychar, near to the parcel of ground that Jacob gave to his son Joseph. Now Jacob's well was there. Jesus therefore, being wearied with his journey, sat thus on the well: and it was about the sixth hour. There cometh a woman of Samaria to draw water: Jesus saith unto her, **Give me to drink.**

Number	Commandment	Context of Commandment
385	*Go, call thy husband, and come hither.*	John 4:9-16 Then saith the woman of Samaria unto him, How is it that thou, being a Jew, askest drink of me, which am a woman of Samaria? for the Jews have no dealings with the Samaritans. Jesus answered and said unto her, If thou knewest the gift of God, and who it is that saith to thee, Give me to drink; thou wouldest have asked of him, and he would have given thee living water. The woman saith unto him, Sir, thou hast nothing to draw with, and the well is deep: from whence then hast thou that living water? Art thou greater than our father Jacob, which gave us the well, and drank thereof himself, and his children, and his cattle? Jesus answered and said unto her, Whosoever drinketh of this water shall thirst again: But whosoever drinketh of the water that I shall give him shall never thirst; but the water that I shall give him shall be in him a well of water springing up into everlasting life. The woman saith unto him, Sir, give me this water, that I thirst not, neither come hither to draw. Jesus saith unto her, **Go, call thy husband, and come hither.**
386	*Woman, believe me, the hour cometh, when ye shall neither in this mountain, nor yet at Jerusalem, worship the Father.*	John 4:19-26 The woman saith unto him, Sir, I perceive that thou art a prophet. Our fathers worshipped in this mountain; and ye say, that in Jerusalem is the place where men ought to worship. Jesus saith unto her, **Woman, believe me, the hour cometh, when ye shall neither in this mountain, nor yet at Jerusalem, worship the Father.** Ye worship ye know not what: we know what we worship: for salvation is of the Jews. But the hour cometh, and now is, when the true worshippers shall worship the Father in spirit and in truth: for the Father seeketh such to worship him. God is a Spirit: and they that worship him must worship him in spirit and in truth. The woman saith unto him, I know that Messias cometh, which is called Christ: when he is come, he will tell us all things. Jesus saith unto her, I that speak unto thee am he.

116

Number	Commandment	Context of Commandment
387	*Lift up your eyes, and look on the fields; for they are white already to harvest.*	John 4:31-38 In the mean while his disciples prayed him, saying, Master, eat. But he said unto them, I have meat to eat that ye know not of. Therefore said the disciples one to another, Hath any man brought him ought to eat? Jesus saith unto them, My meat is to do the will of him that sent me, and to finish his work. Say not ye, There are yet four months, and then cometh harvest? behold, I say unto you, **Lift up your eyes, and look on the fields; for they are white already to harvest.** And he that reapeth receiveth wages, and gathereth fruit unto life eternal: that both he that soweth and he that reapeth may rejoice together. And herein is that saying true, One soweth, and another reapeth. I sent you to reap that whereon ye bestowed no labour: other men laboured, and ye are entered into their labours.
388	*Go thy way; thy son liveth.*	John 4:46-53 So Jesus came again into Cana of Galilee, where he made the water wine. And there was a certain nobleman, whose son was sick at Capernaum. When he heard that Jesus was come out of Judaea into Galilee, he went unto him, and besought him that he would come down, and heal his son: for he was at the point of death. Then said Jesus unto him, Except ye see signs and wonders, ye will not believe. The nobleman saith unto him, Sir, come down ere my child die. Jesus saith unto him, **Go thy way; thy son liveth.** And the man believed the word that Jesus had spoken unto him, and he went his way. And as he was now going down, his servants met him, and told him, saying, Thy son liveth. Then enquired he of them the hour when he began to amend. And they said unto him, Yesterday at the seventh hour the fever left him. So the father knew that it was at the same hour, in the which Jesus said unto him, Thy son liveth: and himself believed, and his whole house.

Number	Commandment	Context of Commandment
389	*Rise, take up thy bed, and walk.*	John 5:2-8 Now there is at Jerusalem by the sheep market a pool, which is called in the Hebrew tongue Bethesda, having five porches. In these lay a great multitude of impotent folk, of blind, halt, withered, waiting for the moving of the water. For an angel went down at a certain season into the pool, and troubled the water: whosoever then first after the troubling of the water stepped in was made whole of whatsoever disease he had. And a certain man was there, which had an infirmity thirty and eight years. When Jesus saw him lie, and knew that he had been now a long time in that case, he saith unto him, Wilt thou be made whole? The impotent man answered him, Sir, I have no man, when the water is troubled, to put me into the pool: but while I am coming, another steppeth down before me. Jesus saith unto him, **Rise, take up thy bed, and walk.**
390	*Behold, thou art made whole:*	John 5:9-14 And immediately the man was made whole, and took up his bed, and walked: and on the same day was the sabbath. The Jews therefore said unto him that was cured, It is the sabbath day: it is not lawful for thee to carry thy bed. He answered them, He that made me whole, the same said unto me, Take up thy bed, and walk. Then asked they him, What man is that which said unto thee, Take up thy bed, and walk? And he that was healed wist not who it was: for Jesus had conveyed himself away, a multitude being in that place. Afterward Jesus findeth him in the temple, and said unto him, **Behold, thou art made whole:** sin no more, lest a worse thing come unto thee.
391	*sin no more, lest a worse thing come unto thee.*	John 5:14-15 Afterward Jesus findeth him in the temple, and said unto him, Behold, thou art made whole: **sin no more, lest a worse thing come unto thee.** The man departed, and told the Jews that it was Jesus, which had made him whole.

Number	Commandment	Context of Commandment
392	*Marvel not at this:*	John 5:25-29 Verily, verily, I say unto you, The hour is coming, and now is, when the dead shall hear the voice of the Son of God: and they that hear shall live. For as the Father hath life in himself; so hath he given to the Son to have life in himself; And hath given him authority to execute judgment also, because he is the Son of man. **Marvel not at this:** for the hour is coming, in the which all that are in the graves shall hear his voice, And shall come forth; they that have done good, unto the resurrection of life; and they that have done evil, unto the resurrection of damnation.
393	*Search the scriptures;*	John 5:32-39 There is another that beareth witness of me; and I know that the witness which he witnesseth of me is true. Ye sent unto John, and he bare witness unto the truth. But I receive not testimony from man: but these things I say, that ye might be saved. He was a burning and a shining light: and ye were willing for a season to rejoice in his light. But I have greater witness than that of John: for the works which the Father hath given me to finish, the same works that I do, bear witness of me, that the Father hath sent me. And the Father himself, which hath sent me, hath borne witness of me. Ye have neither heard his voice at any time, nor seen his shape. And ye have not his word abiding in you: for whom he hath sent, him ye believe not. **Search the scriptures;** for in them ye think ye have eternal life: and they are they which testify of me.

Number	Commandment	Context of Commandment
394	*Do not think that I will accuse you to the Father:*	John 5:43-47 I am come in my Father's name, and ye receive me not: if another shall come in his own name, him ye will receive. How can ye believe, which receive honour one of another, and seek not the honour that cometh from God only? **Do not think that I will accuse you to the Father:** there is one that accuseth you, even Moses, in whom ye trust. For had ye believed Moses, ye would have believed me; for he wrote of me. But if ye believe not his writings, how shall ye believe my words?
395	*Make the men sit down.*	John 6:5-10 When Jesus then lifted up his eyes, and saw a great company come unto him, he saith unto Philip, Whence shall we buy bread, that these may eat? And this he said to prove him: for he himself knew what he would do. Philip answered him, Two hundred pennyworth of bread is not sufficient for them, that every one of them may take a little. One of his disciples, Andrew, Simon Peter's brother, saith unto him, There is a lad here, which hath five barley loaves, and two small fishes: but what are they among so many? And Jesus said, **Make the men sit down.** Now there was much grass in the place. So the men sat down, in number about five thousand.
396	*Gather up the fragments that remain, that nothing be lost.*	John 6:11-13 And Jesus took the loaves; and when he had given thanks, he distributed to the disciples, and the disciples to them that were set down; and likewise of the fishes as much as they would. When they were filled, he said unto his disciples, **Gather up the fragments that remain, that nothing be lost.** Therefore they gathered them together, and filled twelve baskets with the fragments of the five barley loaves, which remained over and above unto them that had eaten.

Number	Commandment	Context of Commandment
397	*Labour not for the meat which perisheth, but for that meat which endureth unto everlasting life, which the Son of man shall give unto you:*	John 6:24-27 When the people therefore saw that Jesus was not there, neither his disciples, they also took shipping, and came to Capernaum, seeking for Jesus. And when they had found him on the other side of the sea, they said unto him, Rabbi, when camest thou hither? Jesus answered them and said, Verily, verily, I say unto you, Ye seek me, not because ye saw the miracles, but because ye did eat of the loaves, and were filled. **Labour not for the meat which perisheth, but for that meat which endureth unto everlasting life, which the Son of man shall give unto you:** for him hath God the Father sealed.
398	*Murmur not among yourselves.*	John 6:41-44 The Jews then murmured at him, because he said, I am the bread which came down from heaven. And they said, Is not this Jesus, the son of Joseph, whose father and mother we know? how is it then that he saith, I came down from heaven? Jesus therefore answered and said unto them, **Murmur not among yourselves.** No man can come to me, except the Father which hath sent me draw him: and I will raise him up at the last day.

Number	Commandment	Context of Commandment
399	*Go ye up unto this feast:*	John 7:3-10 His brethren therefore said unto him, Depart hence, and go into Judaea, that thy disciples also may see the works that thou doest. For there is no man that doeth any thing in secret, and he himself seeketh to be known openly. If thou do these things, shew thyself to the world. For neither did his brethren believe in him. Then Jesus said unto them, My time is not yet come: but your time is alway ready. The world cannot hate you; but me it hateth, because I testify of it, that the works thereof are evil. **Go ye up unto this feast:** I go not up yet unto this feast: for my time is not yet full come. When he had said these words unto them, he abode still in Galilee. But when his brethren were gone up, then went he also up unto the feast, not openly, but as it were in secret.
400	*Judge not according to the appearance, but judge righteous judgment.*	John 7:23-24 If a man on the sabbath day receive circumcision, that the law of Moses should not be broken; are ye angry at me, because I have made a man every whit whole on the sabbath day? **Judge not according to the appearance, but judge righteous judgment.**
401	*If any man thirst, let him come unto me, and drink.*	John 7:37-39 In the last day, that great day of the feast, Jesus stood and cried, saying, **If any man thirst, let him come unto me, and drink.** He that believeth on me, as the scripture hath said, out of his belly shall flow rivers of living water. (But this spake he of the Spirit, which they that believe on him should receive: for the Holy Ghost was not yet given; because that Jesus was not yet glorified.)

Number	Commandment	Context of Commandment
402	*He that is without sin among you, let him first cast a stone at her.*	John 8:3-8 And the scribes and Pharisees brought unto him a woman taken in adultery; and when they had set her in the midst, They say unto him, Master, this woman was taken in adultery, in the very act. Now Moses in the law commanded us, that such should be stoned: but what sayest thou? This they said, tempting him, that they might have to accuse him. But Jesus stooped down, and with his finger wrote on the ground, as though he heard them not. So when they continued asking him, he lifted up himself, and said unto them, **He that is without sin among you, let him first cast a stone at her.** And again he stooped down, and wrote on the ground.
403	*go, and sin no more.*	John 8:9-12 And they which heard it, being convicted by their own conscience, went out one by one, beginning at the eldest, even unto the last: and Jesus was left alone, and the woman standing in the midst. When Jesus had lifted up himself, and saw none but the woman, he said unto her, Woman, where are those thine accusers? hath no man condemned thee? She said, No man, Lord. And Jesus said unto her, Neither do I condemn thee: **go, and sin no more.** Then spake Jesus again unto them, saying, I am the light of the world: he that followeth me shall not walk in darkness, but shall have the light of life.

Number	Commandment	Context of Commandment
404	*Go, wash in the pool of Siloam,*	John 9:1-8 And as Jesus passed by, he saw a man which was blind from his birth. And his disciples asked him, saying, Master, who did sin, this man, or his parents, that he was born blind? Jesus answered, Neither hath this man sinned, nor his parents: but that the works of God should be made manifest in him. I must work the works of him that sent me, while it is day: the night cometh, when no man can work. As long as I am in the world, I am the light of the world. When he had thus spoken, he spat on the ground, and made clay of the spittle, and he anointed the eyes of the blind man with the clay, And said unto him, **Go, wash in the pool of Siloam,** (which is by interpretation, Sent.) He went his way therefore, and washed, and came seeing. The neighbours therefore, and they which before had seen him that he was blind, said, Is not this he that sat and begged?
405	*If I do not the works of my Father, believe me not. But if I do, though ye believe not me, believe the works: that ye may know, and believe, that the Father is in me, and I in him.*	John 10:31-38 Then the Jews took up stones again to stone him. Jesus answered them, Many good works have I shewed you from my Father; for which of those works do ye stone me? The Jews answered him, saying, For a good work we stone thee not; but for blasphemy; and because that thou, being a man, makest thyself God. Jesus answered them, Is it not written in your law, I said, Ye are gods? If he called them gods, unto whom the word of God came, and the scripture cannot be broken; Say ye of him, whom the Father hath sanctified, and sent into the world, Thou blasphemest; because I said, I am the Son of God? **If I do not the works of my Father, believe me not. But if I do, though ye believe not me, believe the works: that ye may know, and believe, that the Father is in me, and I in him.**

Number	Commandment	Context of Commandment
406	*Let us go into Judaea again.*	John 11:6-10 When he had heard therefore that he was sick, he abode two days still in the same place where he was. Then after that saith he to his disciples, **Let us go into Judaea again.** His disciples say unto him, Master, the Jews of late sought to stone thee; and goest thou thither again? Jesus answered, Are there not twelve hours in the day? If any man walk in the day, he stumbleth not, because he seeth the light of this world. But if a man walk in the night, he stumbleth, because there is no light in him.
407	*let us go unto him.*	John 11:11-17 These things said he: and after that he saith unto them, Our friend Lazarus sleepeth; but I go, that I may awake him out of sleep. Then said his disciples, Lord, if he sleep, he shall do well. Howbeit Jesus spake of his death: but they thought that he had spoken of taking of rest in sleep. Then said Jesus unto them plainly, Lazarus is dead. And I am glad for your sakes that I was not there, to the intent ye may believe; nevertheless **let us go unto him.** Then said Thomas, which is called Didymus, unto his fellowdisciples, Let us also go, that we may die with him. Then when Jesus came, he found that he had lain in the grave four days already.
408	*Take ye away the stone.*	John 11:35-40 Jesus wept. Then said the Jews, Behold how he loved him! And some of them said, Could not this man, which opened the eyes of the blind, have caused that even this man should not have died? Jesus therefore again groaning in himself cometh to the grave. It was a cave, and a stone lay upon it. Jesus said, **Take ye away the stone.** Martha, the sister of him that was dead, saith unto him, Lord, by this time he stinketh: for he hath been dead four days. Jesus saith unto her, Said I not unto thee, that, if thou wouldest believe, thou shouldest see the glory of God?

Number	Commandment	Context of Commandment
409	*Lazarus, come forth.*	John 11:41-43 Then they took away the stone from the place where the dead was laid. And Jesus lifted up his eyes, and said, Father, I thank thee that thou hast heard me. And I knew that thou hearest me always: but because of the people which stand by I said it, that they may believe that thou hast sent me. And when he thus had spoken, he cried with a loud voice, **Lazarus, come forth.**
410	*Loose him, and let him go.*	John 11:44-45 And he that was dead came forth, bound hand and foot with graveclothes: and his face was bound about with a napkin. Jesus saith unto them, **Loose him, and let him go.** Then many of the Jews which came to Mary, and had seen the things which Jesus did, believed on him.
411	*If any man serve me, let him follow me;*	John 12:24-26 Verily, verily, I say unto you, Except a corn of wheat fall into the ground and die, it abideth alone: but if it die, it bringeth forth much fruit. He that loveth his life shall lose it; and he that hateth his life in this world shall keep it unto life eternal. **If any man serve me, let him follow me;** and where I am, there shall also my servant be: if any man serve me, him will my Father honour.
412	*Father, glorify thy name.*	John 12:27-30 Now is my soul troubled; and what shall I say? Father, save me from this hour: but for this cause came I unto this hour. **Father, glorify thy name.** Then came there a voice from heaven, saying, I have both glorified it, and will glorify it again. The people therefore, that stood by, and heard it, said that it thundered: others said, An angel spake to him. Jesus answered and said, This voice came not because of me, but for your sakes.

Number	Commandment	Context of Commandment
413	*Walk while ye have the light,*	John 12:31-35 Now is the judgment of this world: now shall the prince of this world be cast out. And I, if I be lifted up from the earth, will draw all men unto me. This he said, signifying what death he should die. The people answered him, We have heard out of the law that Christ abideth for ever: and how sayest thou, The Son of man must be lifted up? who is this Son of man? Then Jesus said unto them, Yet a little while is the light with you. **Walk while ye have the light,** lest darkness come upon you: for he that walketh in darkness knoweth not whither he goeth.
414	*While ye have light, believe in the light,*	John 12:36 **While ye have light, believe in the light,** that ye may be the children of light. These things spake Jesus, and departed, and did hide himself from them.
415	*That thou doest, do quickly.*	John 13:21-27 When Jesus had thus said, he was troubled in spirit, and testified, and said, Verily, verily, I say unto you, that one of you shall betray me. Then the disciples looked one on another, doubting of whom he spake. Now there was leaning on Jesus' bosom one of his disciples, whom Jesus loved. Simon Peter therefore beckoned to him, that he should ask who it should be of whom he spake. He then lying on Jesus' breast saith unto him, Lord, who is it? Jesus answered, He it is, to whom I shall give a sop, when I have dipped it. And when he had dipped the sop, he gave it to Judas Iscariot, the son of Simon. And after the sop Satan entered into him. Then said Jesus unto him, **That thou doest, do quickly.**
416	*love one another; as I have loved you, that ye also love one another.*	John 13:34-35 A new commandment I give unto you, That ye **love one another; as I have loved you, that ye also love one another.** By this shall all men know that ye are my disciples, if ye have love one to another.

Number	Commandment	Context of Commandment
417	*Let not your heart be troubled: ye believe in God, believe also in me.*	John 14:1-3 **Let not your heart be troubled: ye believe in God, believe also in me.** In my Father's house are many mansions: if it were not so, I would have told you. I go to prepare a place for you. And if I go and prepare a place for you, I will come again, and receive you unto myself; that where I am, there ye may be also.
418	*Believe me that I am in the Father, and the Father in me: or else believe me for the very works' sake.*	John 14:6-11 Jesus saith unto him, I am the way, the truth, and the life: no man cometh unto the Father, but by me. If ye had known me, ye should have known my Father also: and from henceforth ye know him, and have seen him. Philip saith unto him, Lord, show us the Father, and it sufficeth us. Jesus saith unto him, Have I been so long time with you, and yet hast thou not known me, Philip? he that hath seen me hath seen the Father; and how sayest thou then, Show us the Father? Believest thou not that I am in the Father, and the Father in me? the words that I speak unto you I speak not of myself: but the Father that dwelleth in me, he doeth the works. **Believe me that I am in the Father, and the Father in me: or else believe me for the very works' sake.**
419	*If ye love me, keep my commandments.*	John 14:15 **If ye love me, keep my commandments.**
420	*Let not your heart be troubled, neither let it be afraid.*	John 14:27 Peace I leave with you, my peace I give unto you: not as the world giveth, give I unto you. **Let not your heart be troubled, neither let it be afraid.**

Number	Commandment	Context of Commandment
421	*Arise, let us go hence.*	John 14:30-31 Hereafter I will not talk much with you: for the prince of this world cometh, and hath nothing in me. But that the world may know that I love the Father; and as the Father gave me commandment, even so I do. **Arise, let us go hence.**
422	*Abide in me, and I in you.*	John 15:1-8 I am the true vine, and my Father is the husbandman. Every branch in me that beareth not fruit he taketh away: and every branch that beareth fruit, he purgeth it, that it may bring forth more fruit. Now ye are clean through the word which I have spoken unto you. **Abide in me, and I in you.** As the branch cannot bear fruit of itself, except it abide in the vine; no more can ye, except ye abide in me. I am the vine, ye are the branches: He that abideth in me, and I in him, the same bringeth forth much fruit: for without me ye can do nothing. If a man abide not in me, he is cast forth as a branch, and is withered; and men gather them, and cast them into the fire, and they are burned. If ye abide in me, and my words abide in you, ye shall ask what ye will, and it shall be done unto you. Herein is my Father glorified, that ye bear much fruit; so shall ye be my disciples.
423	*continue ye in my love.*	John 15:9-11 As the Father hath loved me, so have I loved you: **continue ye in my love.** If ye keep my commandments, ye shall abide in my love; even as I have kept my Father's commandments, and abide in his love. These things have I spoken unto you, that my joy might remain in you, and that your joy might be full.
424	*love one another.*	John 15:17 These things I command you, that ye **love one another.**

Number	Commandment	Context of Commandment
425	*Remember the word that I said unto you, The servant is not greater than his lord.*	John 15:20 **Remember the word that I said unto you, The servant is not greater than his lord.** If they have persecuted me, they will also persecute you; if they have kept my saying, they will keep yours also.
426	*ye asked nothing in my name: ask,*	John 16:24 Hitherto have **ye asked nothing in my name: ask,** and ye shall receive, that your joy may be full.
427	*Behold, the hour cometh, yea, is now come, that ye shall be scattered, every man to his own, and shall leave me alone:*	John 16:32 **Behold, the hour cometh, yea, is now come, that ye shall be scattered, every man to his own, and shall leave me alone:** and yet I am not alone, because the Father is with me.
428	*be of good cheer; I have overcome the world.*	John 16:33 These things I have spoken unto you, that in me ye might have peace. In the world ye shall have tribulation: but **be of good cheer; I have overcome the world.**
429	*Father, the hour is come; glorify thy Son, that thy Son also may glorify thee:*	John 17:1-2 These words spake Jesus, and lifted up his eyes to heaven, and said, **Father, the hour is come; glorify thy Son, that thy Son also may glorify thee:** As thou hast given him power over all flesh, that he should give eternal life to as many as thou hast given him.

Number	Commandment	Context of Commandment
430	*O Father, glorify thou me with thine own self with the glory which I had with thee before the world was.*	John 17:3-5 And this is life eternal, that they might know thee the only true God, and Jesus Christ, whom thou hast sent. I have glorified thee on the earth: I have finished the work which thou gavest me to do. And now, **O Father, glorify thou me with thine own self with the glory which I had with thee before the world was.**
431	*Holy Father, keep through thine own name those whom thou hast given me, that they may be one, as we are.*	John 17:9-11 I pray for them: I pray not for the world, but for them which thou hast given me; for they are thine. And all mine are thine, and thine are mine; and I am glorified in them. And now I am no more in the world, but these are in the world, and I come to thee. **Holy Father, keep through thine own name those whom thou hast given me, that they may be one, as we are.**
432	*Sanctify them through thy truth:*	John 17:15-17 I pray not that thou shouldest take them out of the world, but that thou shouldest keep them from the evil. They are not of the world, even as I am not of the world. **Sanctify them through thy truth:** thy word is truth.
433	*if therefore ye seek me, let these go their way:*	John 18:7-9 Then asked he them again, Whom seek ye? And they said, Jesus of Nazareth. Jesus answered, I have told you that I am he: **if therefore ye seek me, let these go their way:** That the saying might be fulfilled, which he spake, Of them which thou gavest me have I lost none.
434	*Put up thy sword into the sheath:*	John 18:10-11 Then Simon Peter having a sword drew it, and smote the high priest's servant, and cut off his right ear. The servant's name was Malchus. Then said Jesus unto Peter, **Put up thy sword into the sheath:** the cup which my Father hath given me, shall I not drink it?

Number	Commandment	Context of Commandment
435	*ask them which heard me, what I have said unto them: behold, they know what I said.*	John 18:19-21 The high priest then asked Jesus of his disciples, and of his doctrine. Jesus answered him, I spake openly to the world; I ever taught in the synagogue, and in the temple, whither the Jews always resort; and in secret have I said nothing. Why askest thou me? **ask them which heard me, what I have said unto them: behold, they know what I said.**
436	*If I have spoken evil, bear witness of the evil:*	John 18:22-23 And when he had thus spoken, one of the officers which stood by struck Jesus with the palm of his hand, saying, Answerest thou the high priest so? Jesus answered him, **If I have spoken evil, bear witness of the evil:** but if well, why smitest thou me?
437	*Woman, behold thy son!*	John 19:25-26 Now there stood by the cross of Jesus his mother, and his mother's sister, Mary the wife of Cleophas, and Mary Magdalene. When Jesus therefore saw his mother, and the disciple standing by, whom he loved, he saith unto his mother, **Woman, behold thy son!**
438	*Behold thy mother!*	John 19:27 Then saith he to the disciple, **Behold thy mother!** And from that hour that disciple took her unto his own home.
439	*Touch me not; for I am not yet ascended to my Father:*	John 20:16-17 Jesus saith unto her, Mary. She turned herself, and saith unto him, Rabboni; which is to say, Master. Jesus saith unto her, **Touch me not; for I am not yet ascended to my Father:** but go to my brethren, and say unto them, I ascend unto my Father, and your Father; and to my God, and your God.

Number	Commandment	Context of Commandment
440	*go to my brethren, and say unto them, I ascend unto my Father, and your Father; and to my God, and your God.*	John 20:17 Jesus saith unto her, Touch me not; for I am not yet ascended to my Father: but **go to my brethren, and say unto them, I ascend unto my Father, and your Father; and to my God, and your God.**
441	*Receive ye the Holy Ghost:*	John 20:21-23 Then said Jesus to them again, Peace be unto you: as my Father hath sent me, even so send I you. And when he had said this, he breathed on them, and saith unto them, **Receive ye the Holy Ghost:** Whose soever sins ye remit, they are remitted unto them; and whose soever sins ye retain, they are retained.
442	*Reach hither thy finger, and behold my hands; and reach hither thy hand, and thrust it into my side: and be not faithless, but believing.*	John 20:24-29 But Thomas, one of the twelve, called Didymus, was not with them when Jesus came. The other disciples therefore said unto him, We have seen the Lord. But he said unto them, Except I shall see in his hands the print of the nails, and put my finger into the print of the nails, and thrust my hand into his side, I will not believe. And after eight days again his disciples were within, and Thomas with them: then came Jesus, the doors being shut, and stood in the midst, and said, Peace be unto you. Then saith he to Thomas, **Reach hither thy finger, and behold my hands; and reach hither thy hand, and thrust it into my side: and be not faithless, but believing.** And Thomas answered and said unto him, My Lord and my God. Jesus saith unto him, Thomas, because thou hast seen me, thou hast believed: blessed are they that have not seen, and yet have believed.

Number	Commandment	Context of Commandment
443	*Cast the net on the right side of the ship,*	John 21:3-6 Simon Peter saith unto them, I go a fishing. They say unto him, We also go with thee. They went forth, and entered into a ship immediately; and that night they caught nothing. But when the morning was now come, Jesus stood on the shore: but the disciples knew not that it was Jesus. Then Jesus saith unto them, Children, have ye any meat? They answered him, No. And he said unto them, **Cast the net on the right side of the ship,** and ye shall find. They cast therefore, and now they were not able to draw it for the multitude of fishes.
444	*Bring of the fish which ye have now caught.*	John 21:9-11 As soon then as they were come to land, they saw a fire of coals there, and fish laid thereon, and bread. Jesus saith unto them, **Bring of the fish which ye have now caught.** Simon Peter went up, and drew the net to land full of great fishes, an hundred and fifty and three: and for all there were so many, yet was not the net broken.
445	*Come and dine.*	John 21:12-13 Jesus saith unto them, **Come and dine.** And none of the disciples durst ask him, Who art thou? knowing that it was the Lord. Jesus then cometh, and taketh bread, and giveth them, and fish likewise.
446	*Feed my lambs.*	John 21:15 So when they had dined, Jesus saith to Simon Peter, Simon, son of Jonas, lovest thou me more than these? He saith unto him, Yea, Lord; thou knowest that I love thee. He saith unto him, **Feed my lambs.**

Number	Commandment	Context of Commandment
447	*Feed my sheep.*	John 21:16-17 He saith to him again the second time, Simon, son of Jonas, lovest thou me? He saith unto him, Yea, Lord; thou knowest that I love thee. He saith unto him, **Feed my sheep.** He saith unto him the third time, Simon, son of Jonas, lovest thou me? Peter was grieved because he said unto him the third time, Lovest thou me? And he said unto him, Lord, thou knowest all things; thou knowest that I love thee. Jesus saith unto him, Feed my sheep.
448	*Follow me.*	John 21:18-19 Verily, verily, I say unto thee, When thou wast young, thou girdest thyself, and walkedst whither thou wouldest: but when thou shalt be old, thou shalt stretch forth thy hands, and another shall gird thee, and carry thee whither thou wouldest not. This spake he, signifying by what death he should glorify God. And when he had spoken this, he saith unto him, **Follow me.**
449	*follow thou me.*	John 21:20-22 Then Peter, turning about, seeth the disciple whom Jesus loved following; which also leaned on his breast at supper, and said, Lord, which is he that betrayeth thee? Peter seeing him saith to Jesus, Lord, and what shall this man do? Jesus saith unto him, If I will that he tarry till I come, what is that to thee? **follow thou me.**

Commandments
of Jesus Christ
found in:

THE ACTS
OF
THE APOSTLES

Number	Commandment	Context of Commandment
450	*Arise, and go into the city, and it shall be told thee what thou must do.*	Acts 9:4-6 And he fell to the earth, and heard a voice saying unto him, Saul, Saul, why persecutest thou me? And he said, Who art thou, Lord? And the Lord said, I am Jesus whom thou persecutest: it is hard for thee to kick against the pricks. And he trembling and astonished said, Lord, what wilt thou have me to do? And the Lord said unto him, **Arise, and go into the city, and it shall be told thee what thou must do.**
451	*Arise, and go into the street which is called Straight, and enquire in the house of Judas for one called Saul, of Tarsus: for, behold, he prayeth, And hath seen in a vision a man named Ananias coming in, and putting his hand on him, that he might receive his sight.*	Acts 9:11-12 And the Lord said unto him, **Arise, and go into the street which is called Straight, and enquire in the house of Judas for one called Saul, of Tarsus: for, behold, he prayeth, And hath seen in a vision a man named Ananias coming in, and putting his hand on him, that he might receive his sight.**
452	*Go thy way: for he is a chosen vessel unto me, to bear my name before the Gentiles, and kings, and the children of Israel:*	Acts 9:13-16 Then Ananias answered, Lord, I have heard by many of this man, how much evil he hath done to thy saints at Jerusalem: And here he hath authority from the chief priests to bind all that call on thy name. But the Lord said unto him, **Go thy way: for he is a chosen vessel unto me, to bear my name before the Gentiles, and kings, and the children of Israel:** For I will shew him how great things he must suffer for my name's sake.

Number	Commandment	Context of Commandment
453	*Arise, and go into Damascus;*	Acts 22:6-11 And it came to pass, that, as I made my journey, and was come nigh unto Damascus about noon, suddenly there shone from heaven a great light round about me. And I fell unto the ground, and heard a voice saying unto me, Saul, Saul, why persecutest thou me? And I answered, Who art thou, Lord? And he said unto me, I am Jesus of Nazareth, whom thou persecutest. And they that were with me saw indeed the light, and were afraid; but they heard not the voice of him that spake to me. And I said, What shall I do, Lord? And the Lord said unto me, **Arise, and go into Damascus;** and there it shall be told thee of all things which are appointed for thee to do. And when I could not see for the glory of that light, being led by the hand of them that were with me, I came into Damascus.
454	*Make haste, and get thee quickly out of Jerusalem:*	Acts 22:17-18 And it came to pass, that, when I was come again to Jerusalem, even while I prayed in the temple, I was in a trance; And saw him saying unto me, **Make haste, and get thee quickly out of Jerusalem:** for they will not receive thy testimony concerning me.
455	*Depart:*	Acts 22:19-21 And I said, Lord, they know that I imprisoned and beat in every synagogue them that believed on thee: And when the blood of thy martyr Stephen was shed, I also was standing by, and consenting unto his death, and kept the raiment of them that slew him. And he said unto me, **Depart:** for I will send thee far hence unto the Gentiles.

Commandments of Jesus Christ found in: The Acts of The Apostles

Number	Commandment	Context of Commandment
456	*rise, and stand upon thy feet:*	Acts 26:14-18 And when we were all fallen to the earth, I heard a voice speaking unto me, and saying in the Hebrew tongue, Saul, Saul, why persecutest thou me? it is hard for thee to kick against the pricks. And I said, Who art thou, Lord? And he said, I am Jesus whom thou persecutest. But **rise, and stand upon thy feet:** for I have appeared unto thee for this purpose, to make thee a minister and a witness both of these things which thou hast seen, and of those things in the which I will appear unto thee; Delivering thee from the people, and from the Gentiles, unto whom now I send thee, To open their eyes, and to turn them from darkness to light, and from the power of Satan unto God, that they may receive forgiveness of sins, and inheritance among them which are sanctified by faith that is in me.

Commandments
of Jesus Christ
found in:

THE FIRST
EPISTLE OF PAUL
THE APOSTLE
TO THE
CORINTHIANS

Number	Commandment	Context of Commandment
457	*Take, eat: this is my body, which is broken for you: this do in remembrance of me.*	1 Corinthians 11:23-24 For I have received of the Lord that which also I delivered unto you, that the Lord Jesus the same night in which he was betrayed took bread: And when he had given thanks, he brake it, and said, **Take, eat: this is my body, which is broken for you: this do in remembrance of me.**
458	*this cup is the new testament in my blood: this do ye, as oft as ye drink it, in remembrance of me.*	1 Corinthians 11:25 After the same manner also he took the cup, when he had supped, saying, **this cup is the new testament in my blood: this do ye, as oft as ye drink it, in remembrance of me.**

Commandments of Jesus Christ found in:

THE REVELATION OF SAINT JOHN THE DIVINE

We proceed with great caution in documenting the commandments of Jesus Christ from the book of Revelation. We encourage everyone to review the **Entire** book of Revelation.

Number	Commandment	Context of Commandment
459	*What thou seest, write in a book, and send it unto the seven churches which are in Asia; unto Ephesus, and unto Smyrna, and unto Pergamos, and unto Thyatira, and unto Sardis, and unto Philadelphia, and unto Laodicea.*	Revelation 1:10-11 I was in the Spirit on the Lord's day, and heard behind me a great voice, as of a trumpet, Saying, I am Alpha and Omega, the first and the last: and, **What thou seest, write in a book, and send it unto the seven churches which are in Asia; unto Ephesus, and unto Smyrna, and unto Pergamos, and unto Thyatira, and unto Sardis, and unto Philadelphia, and unto Laodicea.**
460	*Fear not; I am the first and the last: I am he that liveth, and was dead;*	Revelation 1:17-18 And when I saw him, I fell at his feet as dead. And he laid his right hand upon me, saying unto me, **Fear not; I am the first and the last: I am he that liveth, and was dead;** and, behold, I am alive for evermore, Amen; and have the keys of hell and of death.
461	*behold, I am alive for evermore,*	Revelation 1:18 I am he that liveth, and was dead; and, **behold, I am alive for evermore,** Amen; and have the keys of hell and of death.
462	*Write the things which thou hast seen, and the things which are, and the things which shall be hereafter;*	Revelation 1:19-20 **Write the things which thou hast seen, and the things which are, and the things which shall be hereafter;** The mystery of the seven stars which thou sawest in my right hand, and the seven golden candlesticks. The seven stars are the angels of the seven churches: and the seven candlesticks which thou sawest are the seven churches.

Number	Commandment	Context of Commandment
463	*Unto the angel of the church of Ephesus write; These things saith he that holdeth the seven stars in his right hand, who walketh in the midst of the seven golden candlesticks; I know thy works, and thy labour, and thy patience, and how thou canst not bear them which are evil: and thou hast tried them which say they are apostles, and are not, and hast found them liars: And hast borne, and hast patience, and for my name's sake hast laboured, and hast not fainted. Nevertheless I have somewhat against thee, because thou hast left thy first love. Remember therefore from whence thou art fallen, and repent, and do the first works; or else I will come unto thee quickly, and will remove thy candlestick out of his place, except thou repent. But this thou hast, that thou hatest the deeds of the Nicolaitanes, which I also hate.*	Revelation 2:1-6 Unto the angel of the church of Ephesus write; These things saith he that holdeth the seven stars in his right hand, who walketh in the midst of the seven golden candlesticks; I know thy works, and thy labour, and thy patience, and how thou canst not bear them which are evil: and thou hast tried them which say they are apostles, and are not, and hast found them liars: And hast borne, and hast patience, and for my name's sake hast laboured, and hast not fainted. Nevertheless I have somewhat against thee, because thou hast left thy first love. Remember therefore from whence thou art fallen, and repent, and do the first works; or else I will come unto thee quickly, and will remove thy candlestick out of his place, except thou repent. But this thou hast, that thou hatest the deeds of the Nicolaitanes, which I also hate.

144

Number	Commandment	Context of Commandment
464	*Remember therefore from whence thou art fallen, and repent, and do the first works;*	Revelation 2:5 **Remember therefore from whence thou art fallen, and repent, and do the first works;** or else I will come unto thee quickly, and will remove thy candlestick out of his place, except thou repent.
465	*He that hath an ear, let him hear what the Spirit saith unto the churches;*	Revelation 2:7 **He that hath an ear, let him hear what the Spirit saith unto the churches;** To him that overcometh will I give to eat of the tree of life, which is in the midst of the paradise of God.
466	*unto the angel of the church in Smyrna write; These things saith the first and the last, which was dead, and is alive; I know thy works, and tribulation, and poverty, (but thou art rich) and I know the blasphemy of them which say they are Jews, and are not, but are the synagogue of Satan. Fear none of those things which thou shalt suffer: behold, the devil shall cast some of you into prison, that ye may be tried; and ye shall have tribulation ten days: be thou faithful unto death, and I will give thee a crown of life.*	Revelation 2:8-10 And **unto the angel of the church in Smyrna write; These things saith the first and the last, which was dead, and is alive; I know thy works, and tribulation, and poverty, (but thou art rich) and I know the blasphemy of them which say they are Jews, and are not, but are the synagogue of Satan. Fear none of those things which thou shalt suffer: behold, the devil shall cast some of you into prison, that ye may be tried; and ye shall have tribulation ten days: be thou faithful unto death, and I will give thee a crown of life.**

Number	Commandment	Context of Commandment
467	*Fear none of those things which thou shalt suffer:*	Revelation 2:10 **Fear none of those things which thou shalt suffer:** behold, the devil shall cast some of you into prison, that ye may be tried; and ye shall have tribulation ten days: be thou faithful unto death, and I will give thee a crown of life.
468	*behold, the devil shall cast some of you into prison, that ye may be tried; and ye shall have tribulation ten days:*	Revelation 2:10 Fear none of those things which thou shalt suffer: **behold, the devil shall cast some of you into prison, that ye may be tried; and ye shall have tribulation ten days:** be thou faithful unto death, and I will give thee a crown of life.
469	*be thou faithful unto death,*	Revelation 2:10 Fear none of those things which thou shalt suffer: behold, the devil shall cast some of you into prison, that ye may be tried; and ye shall have tribulation ten days: **be thou faithful unto death,** and I will give thee a crown of life.
470	*He that hath an ear, let him hear what the Spirit saith unto the churches;*	Revelation 2:11 **He that hath an ear, let him hear what the Spirit saith unto the churches;** He that overcometh shall not be hurt of the second death.

Number	Commandment	Context of Commandment

471 *to the angel of the church in Pergamos write; These things saith he which hath the sharp sword with two edges; I know thy works, and where thou dwellest, even where Satan's seat is: and thou holdest fast my name, and hast not denied my faith, even in those days wherein Antipas was my faithful martyr, who was slain among you, where Satan dwelleth. But I have a few things against thee, because thou hast there them that hold the doctrine of Balaam, who taught Balac to cast a stumblingblock before the children of Israel, to eat things sacrificed unto idols, and to commit fornication. So hast thou also them that hold the doctrine of the Nicolaitanes, which thing I hate. Repent; or else I will come unto thee quickly, and will fight against them with the sword of my mouth.*

Revelation 2:12-16
And **to the angel of the church in Pergamos write; These things saith he which hath the sharp sword with two edges; I know thy works, and where thou dwellest, even where Satan's seat is: and thou holdest fast my name, and hast not denied my faith, even in those days wherein Antipas was my faithful martyr, who was slain among you, where Satan dwelleth. But I have a few things against thee, because thou hast there them that hold the doctrine of Balaam, who taught Balac to cast a stumblingblock before the children of Israel, to eat things sacrificed unto idols, and to commit fornication. So hast thou also them that hold the doctrine of the Nicolaitanes, which thing I hate. Repent; or else I will come unto thee quickly, and will fight against them with the sword of my mouth.**

Number	Commandment	Context of Commandment
472	*Repent;*	Revelation 2:16 **Repent;** or else I will come unto thee quickly, and will fight against them with the sword of my mouth.
473	*He that hath an ear, let him hear what the Spirit saith unto the churches;*	Revelation 2:17 **He that hath an ear, let him hear what the Spirit saith unto the churches;** To him that overcometh will I give to eat of the hidden manna, and will give him a white stone, and in the stone a new name written, which no man knoweth saving he that receiveth it.

148

Number	Commandment	Context of Commandment

474

unto the angel of the church in Thyatira write; These things saith the Son of God, who hath his eyes like unto a flame of fire, and his feet are like fine brass; I know thy works, and charity, and service, and faith, and thy patience, and thy works; and the last to be more than the first. Notwithstanding I have a few things against thee, because thou sufferest that woman Jezebel, which calleth herself a prophetess, to teach and to seduce my servants to commit fornication, and to eat things sacrificed unto idols. And I gave her space to repent of her fornication; and she repented not. Behold, I will cast her into a bed, and them that commit adultery with her into great tribulation, except they repent of their deeds. And I will kill her children with death; and all the churches shall know that I am he which searcheth the reins and hearts: and I will give unto every one of you according to your works. But unto you I say, and unto the rest in Thyatira, as many as have not this doctrine, and which have not known the depths of Satan, as they speak; I will put upon you none other burden. But that which ye have already hold fast till I come. And he that overcometh, and keepeth my works unto the end, to him will I give power over the nations: And he shall rule them with a rod of iron; as the vessels of a potter shall they be broken to shivers: even as I received of my Father. And I will give him the morning star. He that hath an ear, let him hear what the Spirit saith unto the churches.

Revelation 2:18-29

And **unto the angel of the church in Thyatira write; These things saith the Son of God, who hath his eyes like unto a flame of fire, and his feet are like fine brass; I know thy works, and charity, and service, and faith, and thy patience, and thy works; and the last to be more than the first. Notwithstanding I have a few things against thee, because thou sufferest that woman Jezebel, which calleth herself a prophetess, to teach and to seduce my servants to commit fornication, and to eat things sacrificed unto idols. And I gave her space to repent of her fornication; and she repented not. Behold, I will cast her into a bed, and them that commit adultery with her into great tribulation, except they repent of their deeds. And I will kill her children with death; and all the churches shall know that I am he which searcheth the reins and hearts: and I will give unto every one of you according to your works. But unto you I say, and unto the rest in Thyatira, as many as have not this doctrine, and which have not known the depths of Satan, as they speak; I will put upon you none other burden. But that which ye have already hold fast till I come. And he that overcometh, and keepeth my works unto the end, to him will I give power over the nations: And he shall rule them with a rod of iron; as the vessels of a potter shall they be broken to shivers: even as I received of my Father. And I will give him the morning star. He that hath an ear, let him hear what the Spirit saith unto the churches.**

Number	Commandment	Context of Commandment
475	*Behold, I will cast her into a bed, and them that commit adultery with her into great tribulation, except they repent of their deeds.*	Revelation 2:20-23 Notwithstanding I have a few things against thee, because thou sufferest that woman Jezebel, which calleth herself a prophetess, to teach and to seduce my servants to commit fornication, and to eat things sacrificed unto idols. And I gave her space to repent of her fornication; and she repented not. **Behold, I will cast her into a bed, and them that commit adultery with her into great tribulation, except they repent of their deeds.** And I will kill her children with death; and all the churches shall know that I am he which searcheth the reins and hearts: and I will give unto every one of you according to your works.
476	*that which ye have already hold fast till I come.*	Revelation 2:24-25 But unto you I say, and unto the rest in Thyatira, as many as have not this doctrine, and which have not known the depths of Satan, as they speak; I will put upon you none other burden. But **that which ye have already hold fast till I come.**

Number	Commandment	Context of Commandment

477

unto the angel of the church in Sardis write; These things saith he that hath the seven Spirits of God, and the seven stars; I know thy works, that thou hast a name that thou livest, and art dead. Be watchful, and strengthen the things which remain, that are ready to die: for I have not found thy works perfect before God. Remember therefore how thou hast received and heard, and hold fast, and repent. If therefore thou shalt not watch, I will come on thee as a thief, and thou shalt not know what hour I will come upon thee. Thou hast a few names even in Sardis which have not defiled their garments; and they shall walk with me in white: for they are worthy. He that overcometh, the same shall be clothed in white raiment; and I will not blot out his name out of the book of life, but I will confess his name before my Father, and before his angels. He that hath an ear, let him hear what the Spirit saith unto the churches.

Revelation 3:1-6
And **unto the angel of the church in Sardis write; These things saith he that hath the seven Spirits of God, and the seven stars; I know thy works, that thou hast a name that thou livest, and art dead. Be watchful, and strengthen the things which remain, that are ready to die: for I have not found thy works perfect before God. Remember therefore how thou hast received and heard, and hold fast, and repent. If therefore thou shalt not watch, I will come on thee as a thief, and thou shalt not know what hour I will come upon thee. Thou hast a few names even in Sardis which have not defiled their garments; and they shall walk with me in white: for they are worthy. He that overcometh, the same shall be clothed in white raiment; and I will not blot out his name out of the book of life, but I will confess his name before my Father, and before his angels. He that hath an ear, let him hear what the Spirit saith unto the churches.**

Number	Commandment	Context of Commandment
478	*Be watchful, and strengthen the things which remain, that are ready to die:*	Revelation 3:2 **Be watchful, and strengthen the things which remain, that are ready to die:** for I have not found thy works perfect before God.
479	*Remember therefore how thou hast received and heard, and hold fast, and repent.*	Revelation 3:3 **Remember therefore how thou hast received and heard, and hold fast, and repent.** If therefore thou shalt not watch, I will come on thee as a thief, and thou shalt not know what hour I will come upon thee.

Number	Commandment	Context of Commandment

to the angel of the church in Philadelphia write; These things saith he that is holy, he that is true, he that hath the key of David, he that openeth, and no man shutteth; and shutteth, and no man openeth; I know thy works: behold, I have set before thee an open door, and no man can shut it: for thou hast a little strength, and hast kept my word, and hast not denied my name. Behold, I will make them of the synagogue of Satan, which say they are Jews, and are not, but do lie; behold, I will make them to come and worship before thy feet, and to know that I have loved thee.

480 *Because thou hast kept the word of my patience, I also will keep thee from the hour of temptation, which shall come upon all the world, to try them that dwell upon the earth. Behold, I come quickly: hold that fast which thou hast, that no man take thy crown. Him that overcometh will I make a pillar in the temple of my God, and he shall go no more out: and I will write upon him the name of my God, and the name of the city of my God, which is new Jerusalem, which cometh down out of heaven from my God: and I will write upon him my new name. He that hath an ear, let him hear what the Spirit saith unto the churches.*

Revelation 3:7-13
And **to the angel of the church in Philadelphia write; These things saith he that is holy, he that is true, he that hath the key of David, he that openeth, and no man shutteth; and shutteth, and no man openeth; I know thy works: behold, I have set before thee an open door, and no man can shut it: for thou hast a little strength, and hast kept my word, and hast not denied my name. Behold, I will make them of the synagogue of Satan, which say they are Jews, and are not, but do lie; behold, I will make them to come and worship before thy feet, and to know that I have loved thee. Because thou hast kept the word of my patience, I also will keep thee from the hour of temptation, which shall come upon all the world, to try them that dwell upon the earth. Behold, I come quickly: hold that fast which thou hast, that no man take thy crown. Him that overcometh will I make a pillar in the temple of my God, and he shall go no more out: and I will write upon him the name of my God, and the name of the city of my God, which is new Jerusalem, which cometh down out of heaven from my God: and I will write upon him my new name. He that hath an ear, let him hear what the Spirit saith unto the churches.**

Number	Commandment	Context of Commandment
481	*behold, I have set before thee an open door, and no man can shut it:*	Revelation 3:8 I know thy works: **behold, I have set before thee an open door, and no man can shut it:** for thou hast a little strength, and hast kept my word, and hast not denied my name.
482	*Behold, I will make them of the synagogue of Satan, which say they are Jews, and are not, but do lie;*	Revelation 3:9 **Behold, I will make them of the synagogue of Satan, which say they are Jews, and are not, but do lie;** behold, I will make them to come and worship before thy feet, and to know that I have loved thee.
483	*behold, I will make them to come and worship before thy feet, and to know that I have loved thee.*	Revelation 3:9 Behold, I will make them of the synagogue of Satan, which say they are Jews, and are not, but do lie; **behold, I will make them to come and worship before thy feet, and to know that I have loved thee.**
484	*Behold, I come quickly:*	Revelation 3:11 **Behold, I come quickly:** hold that fast which thou hast, that no man take thy crown.
485	*hold that fast which thou hast,*	Revelation 3:11 Behold, I come quickly: **hold that fast which thou hast,** that no man take thy crown.

Number	Commandment	Context of Commandment

unto the angel of the church of the Laodiceans write; These things saith the Amen, the faithful and true witness, the beginning of the creation of God; I know thy works, that thou art neither cold nor hot: I would thou wert cold or hot. So then because thou art lukewarm, and neither cold nor hot, I will spue thee out of my mouth. Because thou sayest, I am rich, and increased with goods, and have need of nothing; and knowest not that thou art wretched, and miserable, and poor, and blind, and naked: I counsel thee to buy of me gold

486 *tried in the fire, that thou mayest be rich; and white raiment, that thou mayest be clothed, and that the shame of thy nakedness do not appear; and anoint thine eyes with eyesalve, that thou mayest see. As many as I love, I rebuke and chasten: be zealous therefore, and repent. Behold, I stand at the door, and knock: if any man hear my voice, and open the door, I will come in to him, and will sup with him, and he with me. To him that overcometh will I grant to sit with me in my throne, even as I also overcame, and am set down with my Father in his throne. He that hath an ear, let him hear what the Spirit saith unto the churches.*

Revelation 3:14-22
And **unto the angel of the church of the Laodiceans write; These things saith the Amen, the faithful and true witness, the beginning of the creation of God; I know thy works, that thou art neither cold nor hot: I would thou wert cold or hot. So then because thou art lukewarm, and neither cold nor hot, I will spue thee out of my mouth. Because thou sayest, I am rich, and increased with goods, and have need of nothing; and knowest not that thou art wretched, and miserable, and poor, and blind, and naked: I counsel thee to buy of me gold tried in the fire, that thou mayest be rich; and white raiment, that thou mayest be clothed, and that the shame of thy nakedness do not appear; and anoint thine eyes with eyesalve, that thou mayest see. As many as I love, I rebuke and chasten: be zealous therefore, and repent. Behold, I stand at the door, and knock: if any man hear my voice, and open the door, I will come in to him, and will sup with him, and he with me. To him that overcometh will I grant to sit with me in my throne, even as I also overcame, and am set down with my Father in his throne. He that hath an ear, let him hear what the Spirit saith unto the churches.**

Number	Commandment	Context of Commandment
487	*be zealous therefore, and repent.*	Revelation 3:19 As many as I love, I rebuke and chasten: **be zealous therefore, and repent.**
488	*Behold, I stand at the door, and knock:*	Revelation 3:20 **Behold, I stand at the door, and knock:** if any man hear my voice, and open the door, I will come in to him, and will sup with him, and he with me.
489	*Behold, I come as a thief.*	Revelation 16:15 **Behold, I come as a thief.** Blessed is he that watcheth, and keepeth his garments, lest he walk naked, and they see his shame.
490	*Behold, I come quickly:*	Revelation 22:7 **Behold, I come quickly:** blessed is he that keepeth the sayings of the prophecy of this book.
491	*behold, I come quickly;*	Revelation 22:12 And, **behold, I come quickly;** and my reward is with me, to give every man according as his work shall be.

THE END

AFTERWORD

If you have made it through this book and are excited to Keep the Commandments of Jesus Christ, we invite you to visit www.UnitedInJesusChrist.org to play an active role in helping Unite the people of God worldwide by adding yourself to the United In Jesus Christ Global Directory.

When you do this, you will be able to connect with other followers of Jesus Christ locally and globally who have also learned the Commandments of Jesus Christ and are committed to living them.

Jesus is recorded saying:

"Therefore whosoever heareth these sayings of mine, and doeth them, I will liken him unto a wise man, which built his house upon a rock: and the rain descended, and the floods came, and the winds blew, and beat upon that house; and it fell not: for it was founded upon a rock. And every one that heareth these sayings of mine, and doeth them not, shall be likened unto a foolish man, which built his house upon the sand: and the rain descended, and the floods came, and the winds blew, and beat upon that house; and it fell: and great was the fall of it."
Matthew 7:24-27

As recorded in the Gospel according to John chapter 14 Jesus said;

"He that hath my commandments, and keepeth them, he it is that loveth me: and he that loveth me shall be loved of my Father, and I will love him, and will manifest myself to him."
John 14:21

As recorded in the Gospel according to John chapter 15 Jesus said;

"As the Father hath loved me, so have I loved you: continue ye in my love. If ye keep my commandments, ye shall abide in my love; even as I have kept my Father's commandments, and abide in his love."
John 15:9-10

In the first chapter of 2 John it is written:

"Whosoever transgresseth, and abideth not in the doctrine of Christ, hath not God. He that abideth in the doctrine of Christ, he hath both the Father and the Son. If there come any unto you, and bring not this doctrine, receive him not into your house, neither bid him God speed: for he that biddeth him God speed is partaker of his evil deeds."
2 John 1:9-11

If you have any questions, concerns, comments, or suggestions contact us at:
info@UnitedInJesusChrist.org

or write us at:

**United In Jesus Christ
PO Box 563
Yucaipa California 92399
USA**